This book belongs to

....

....

....

....

....

....

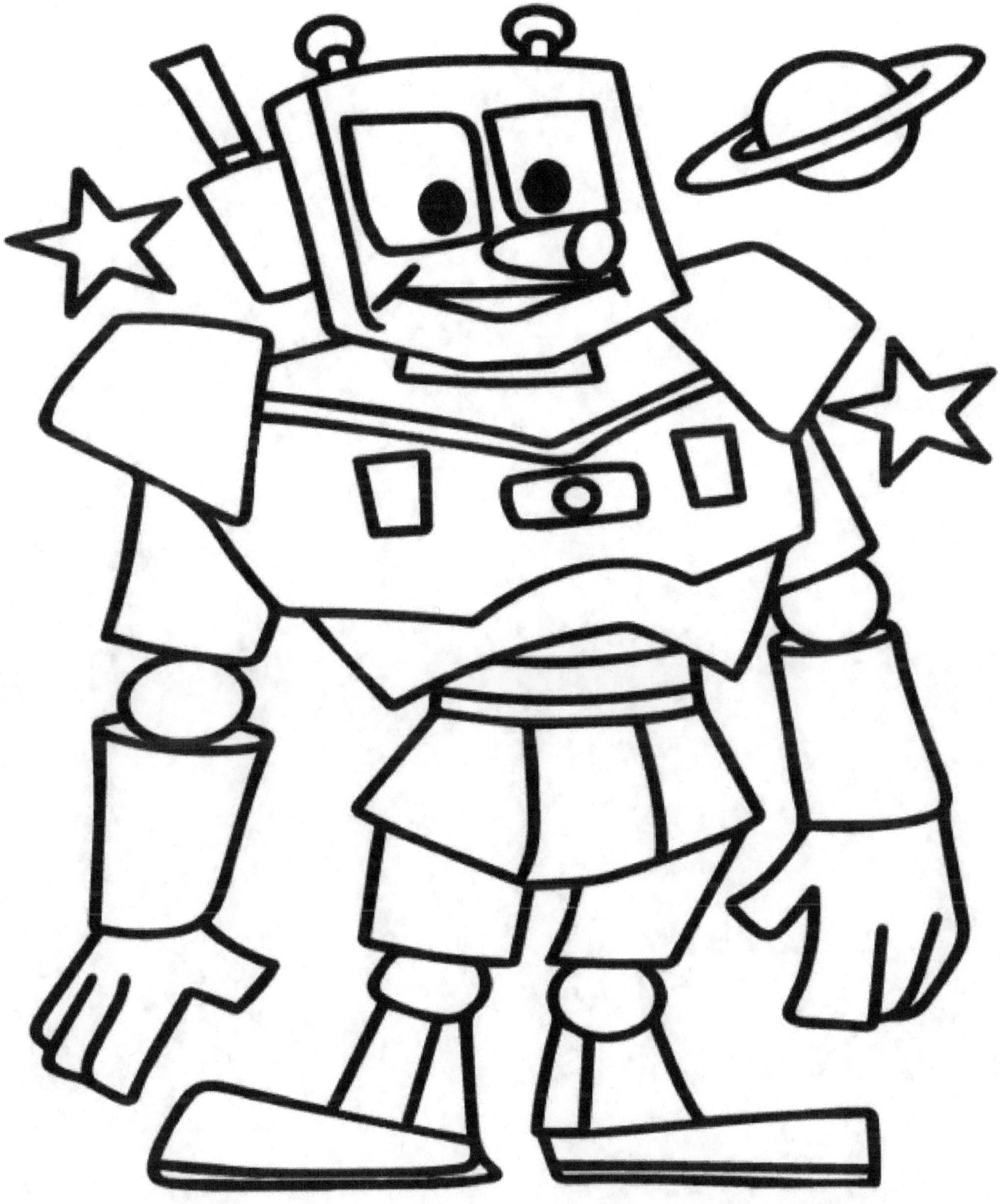

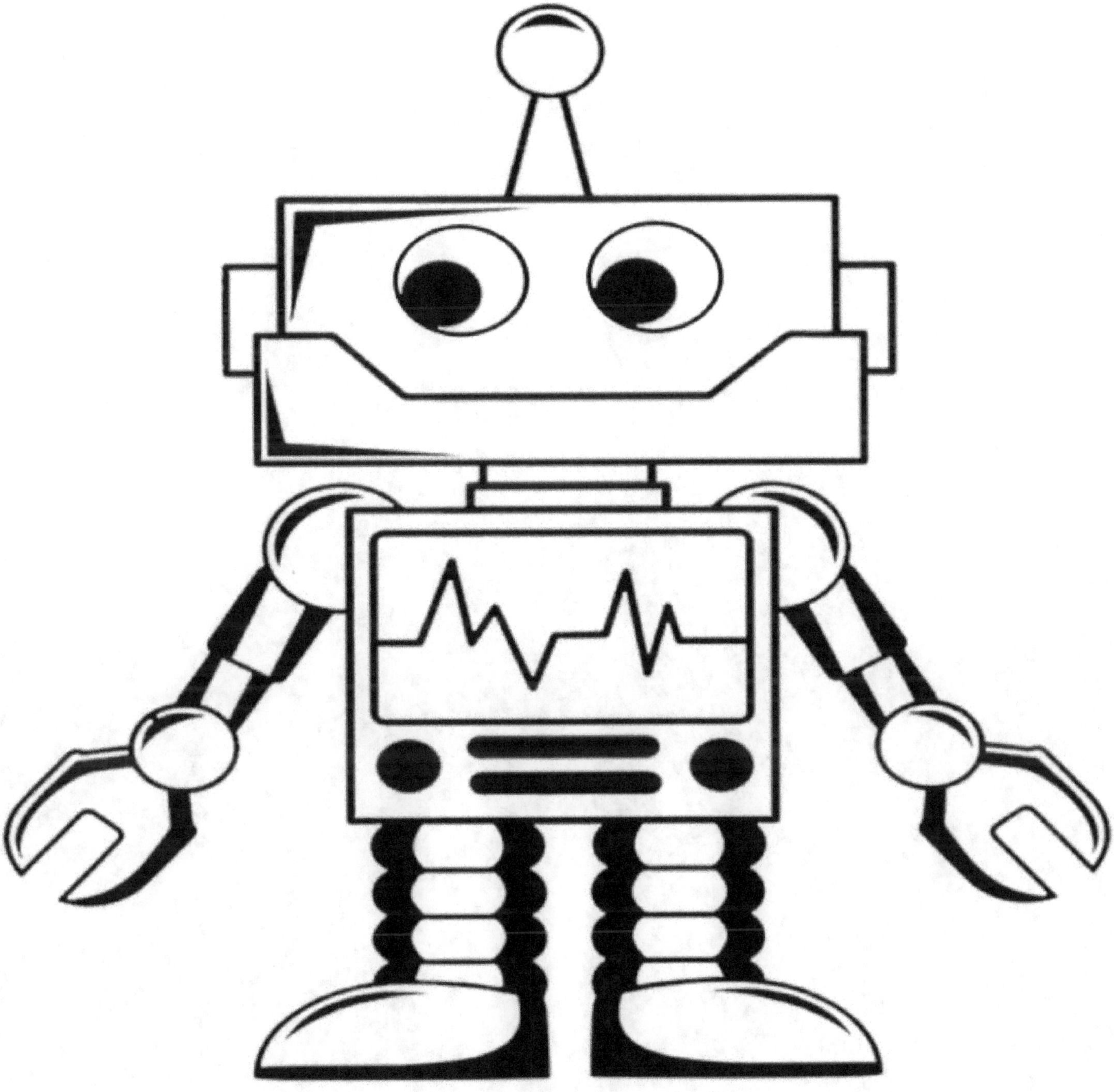

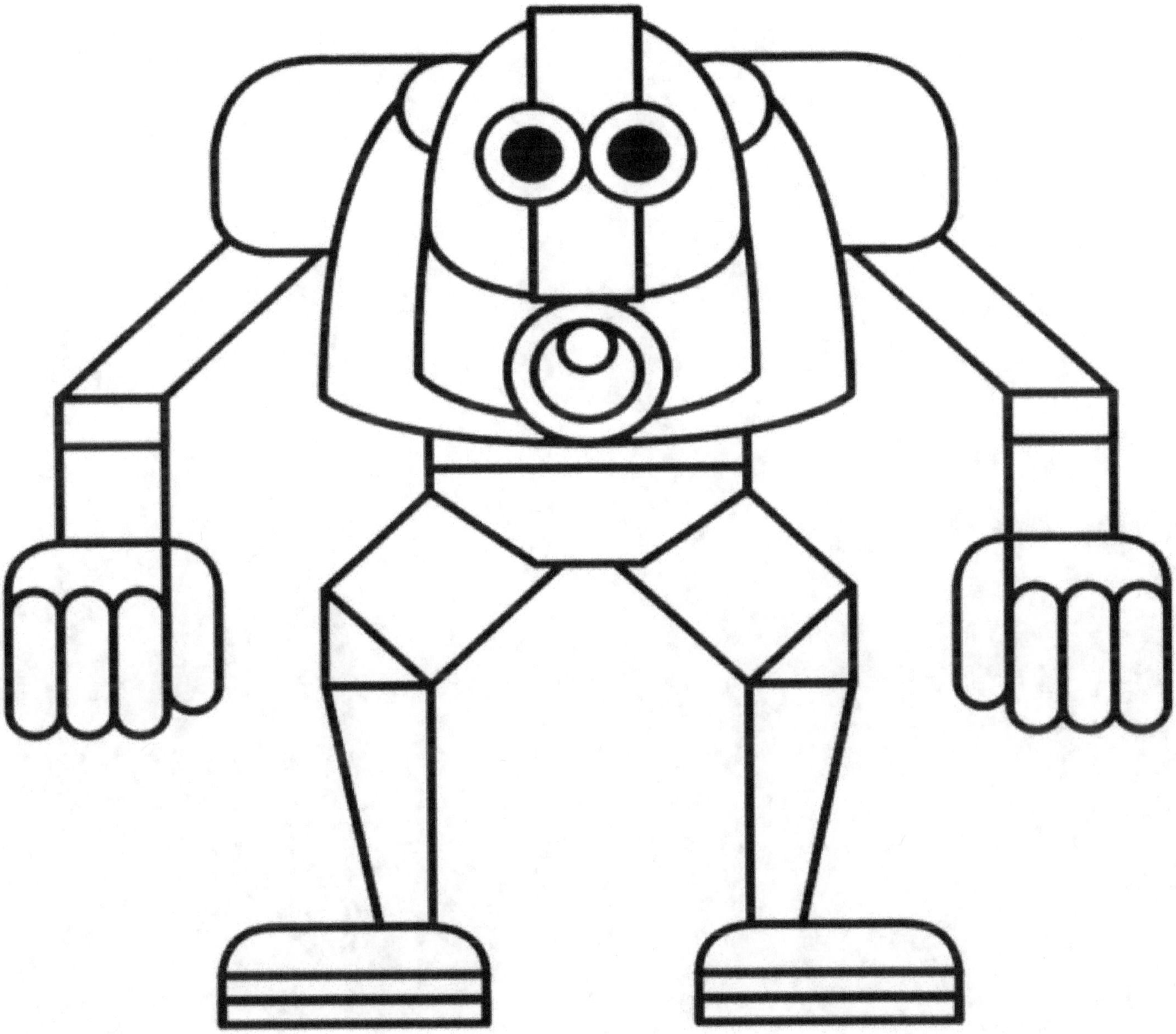

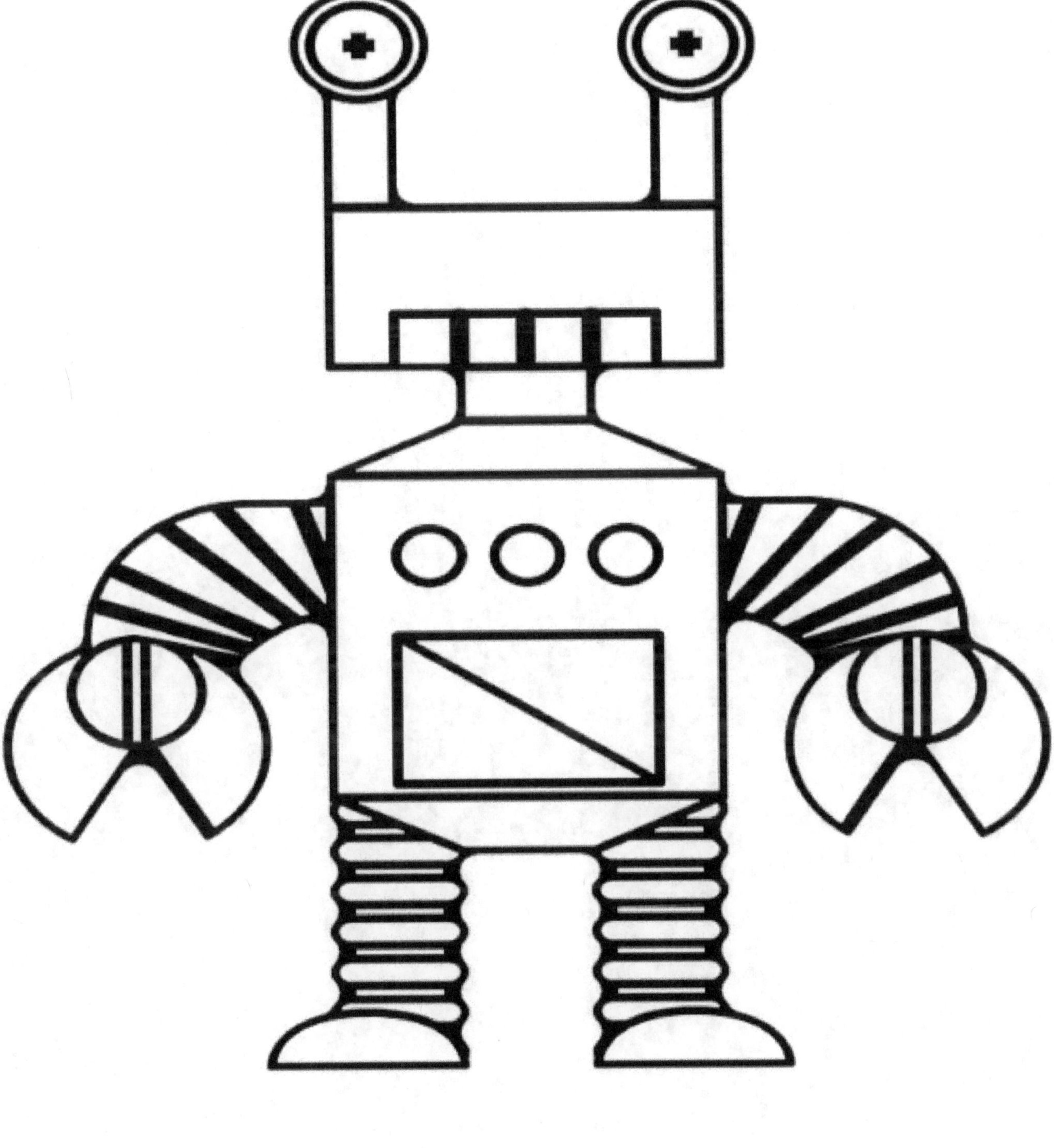

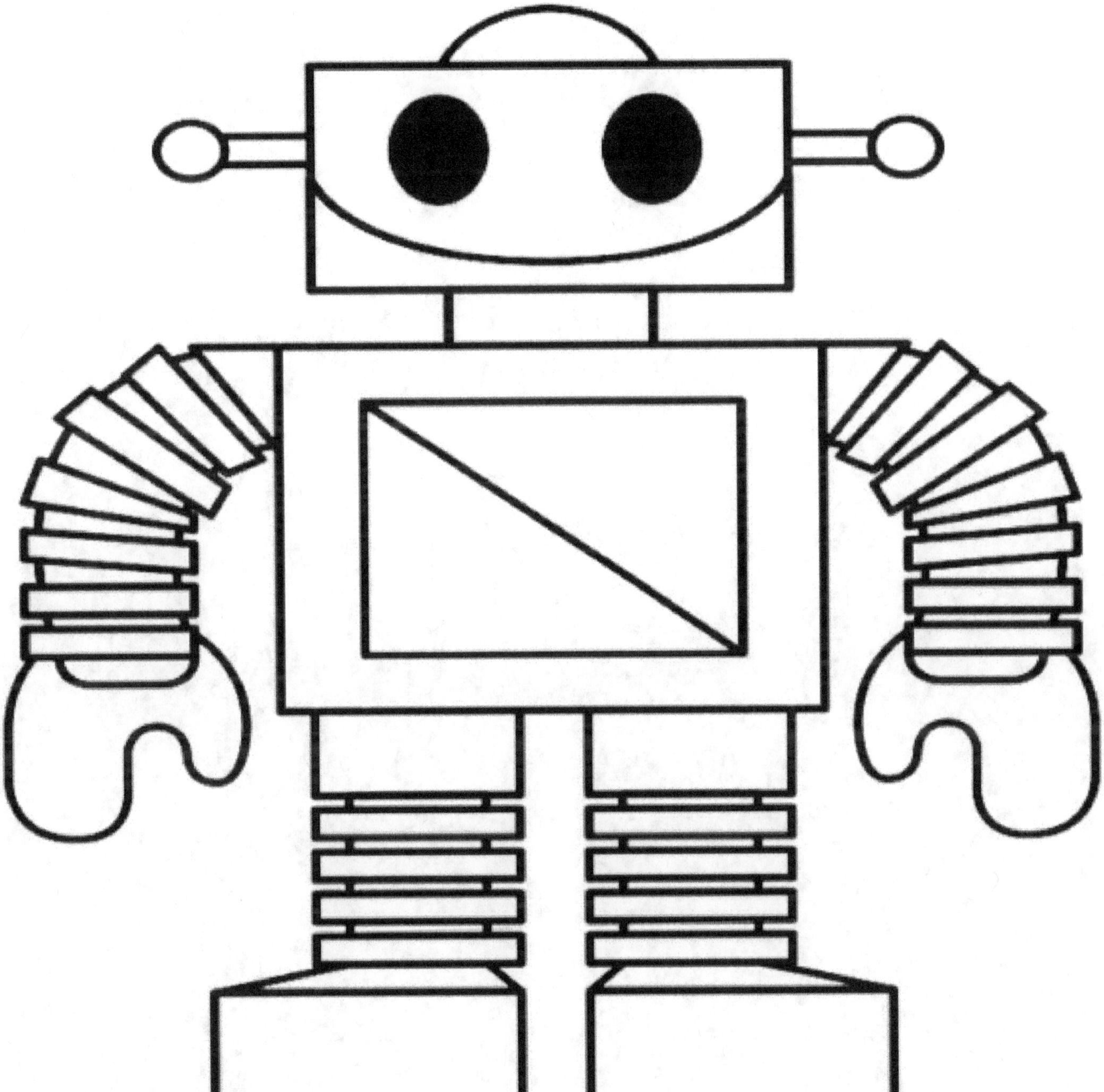

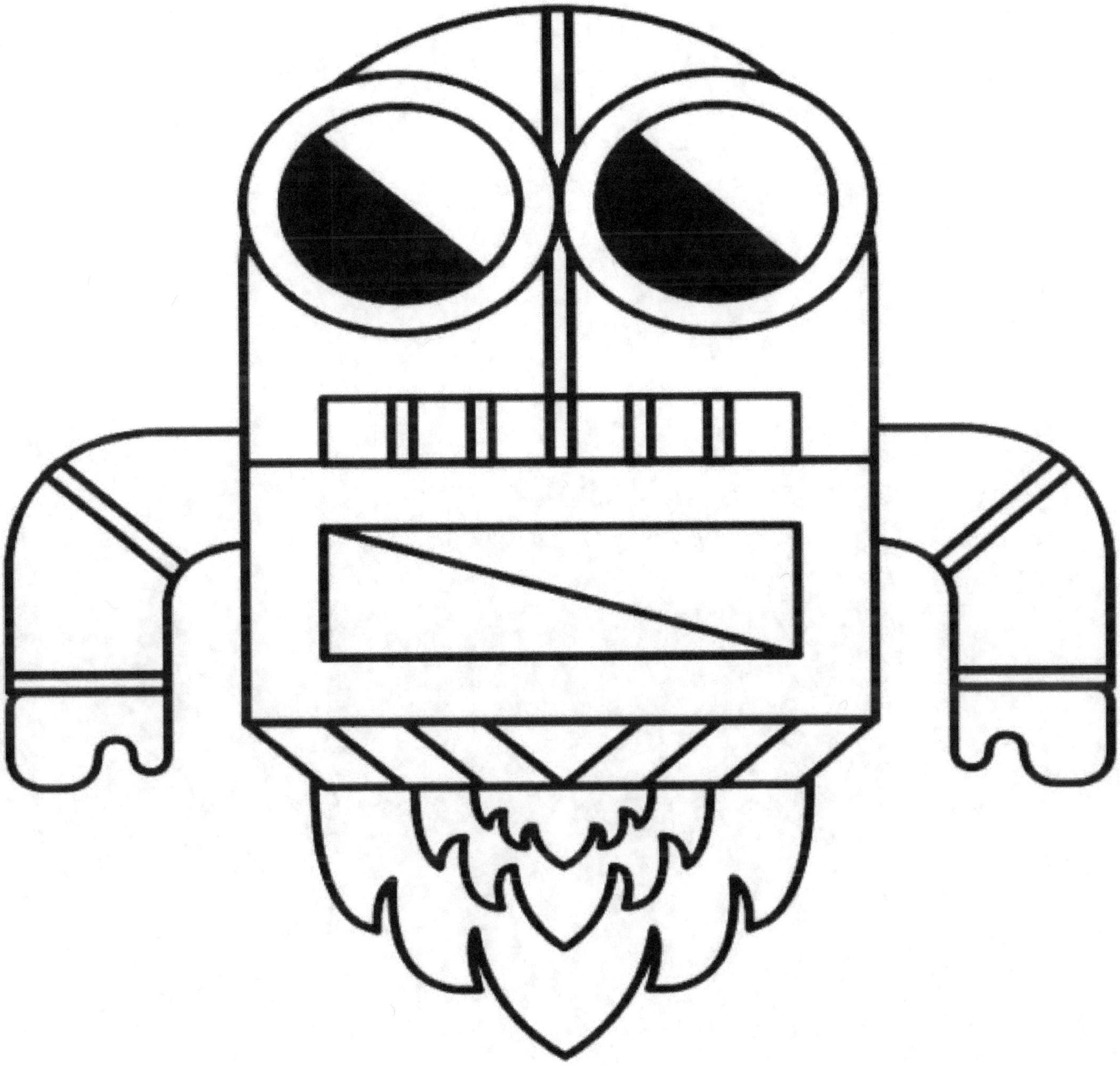

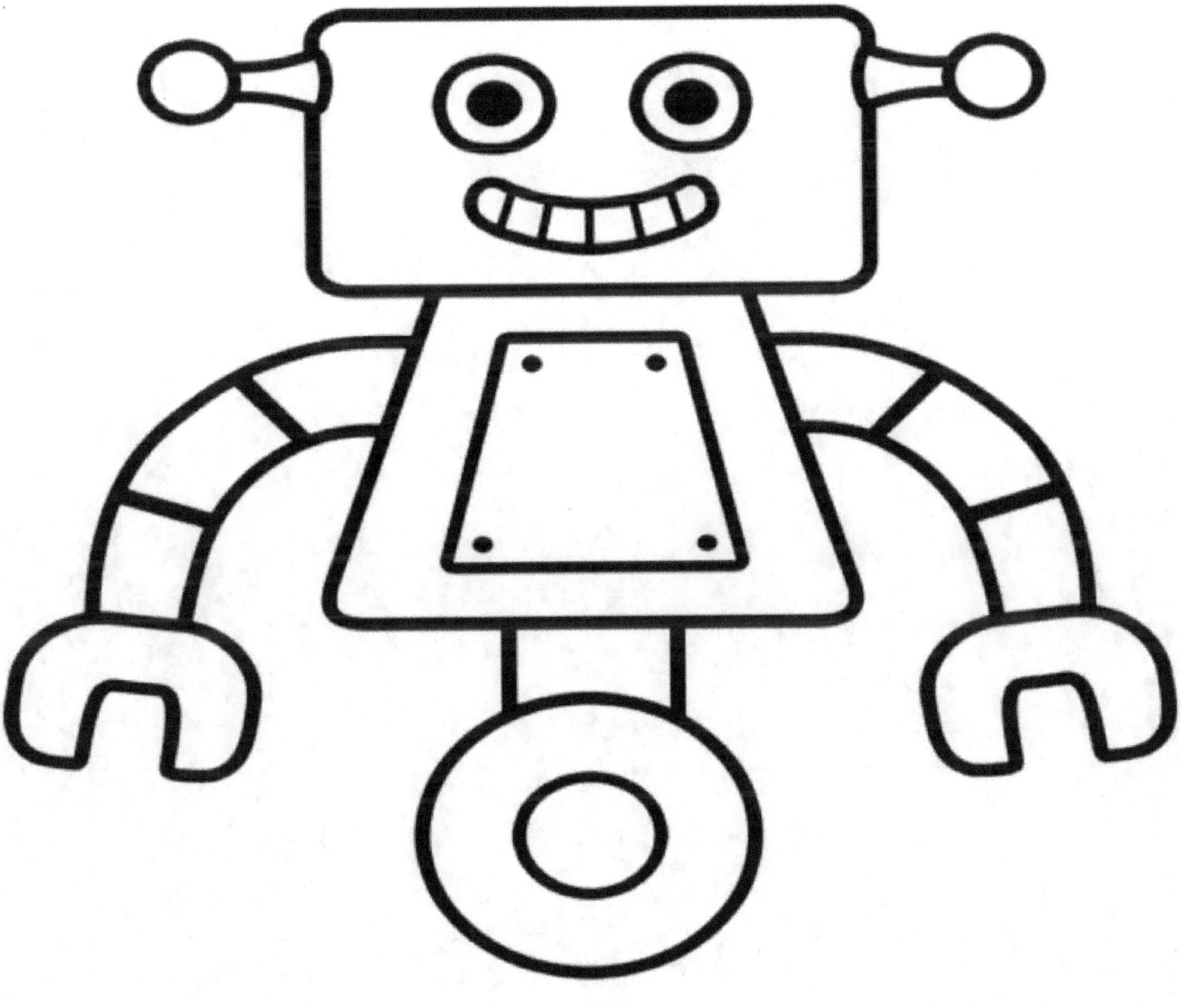

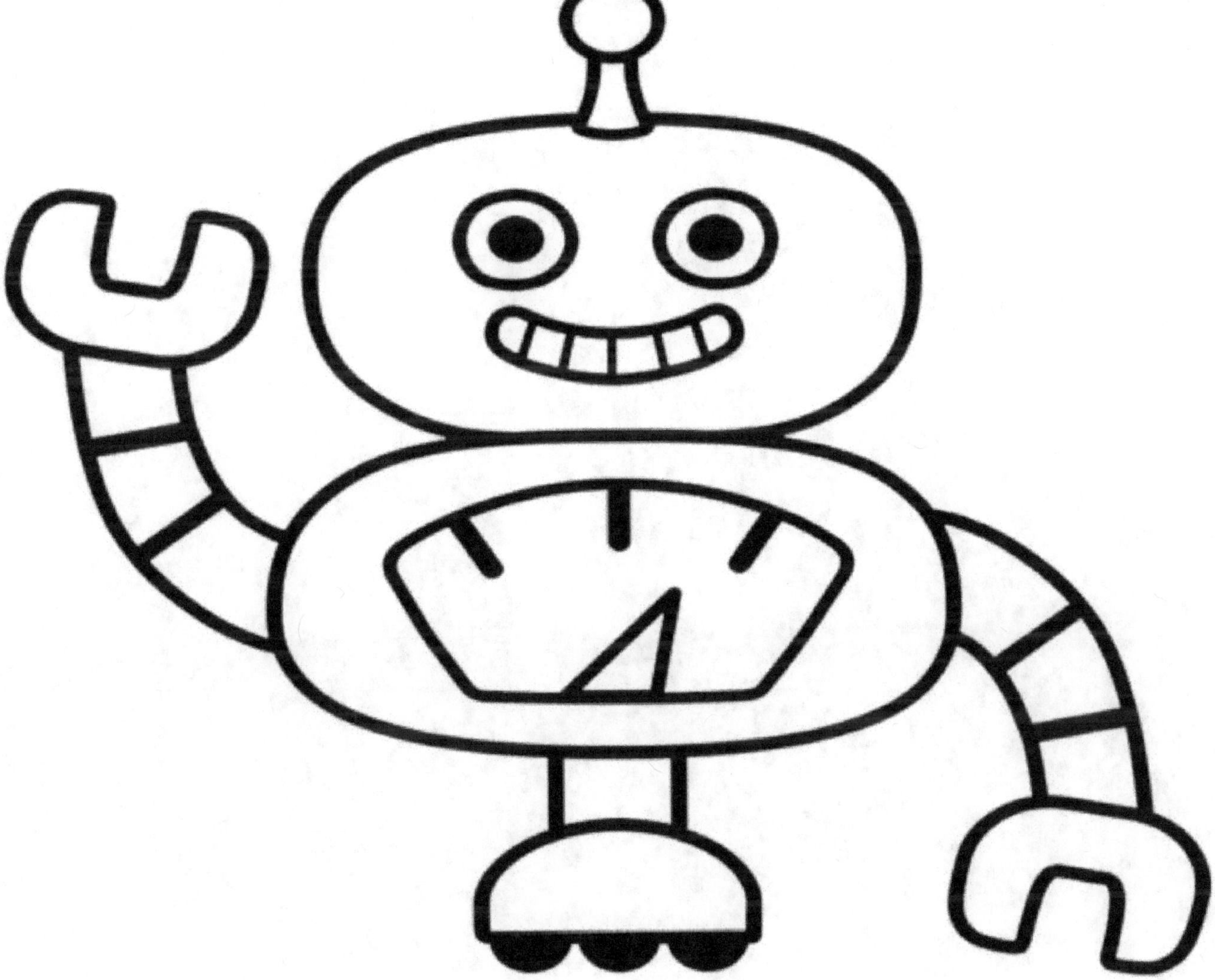

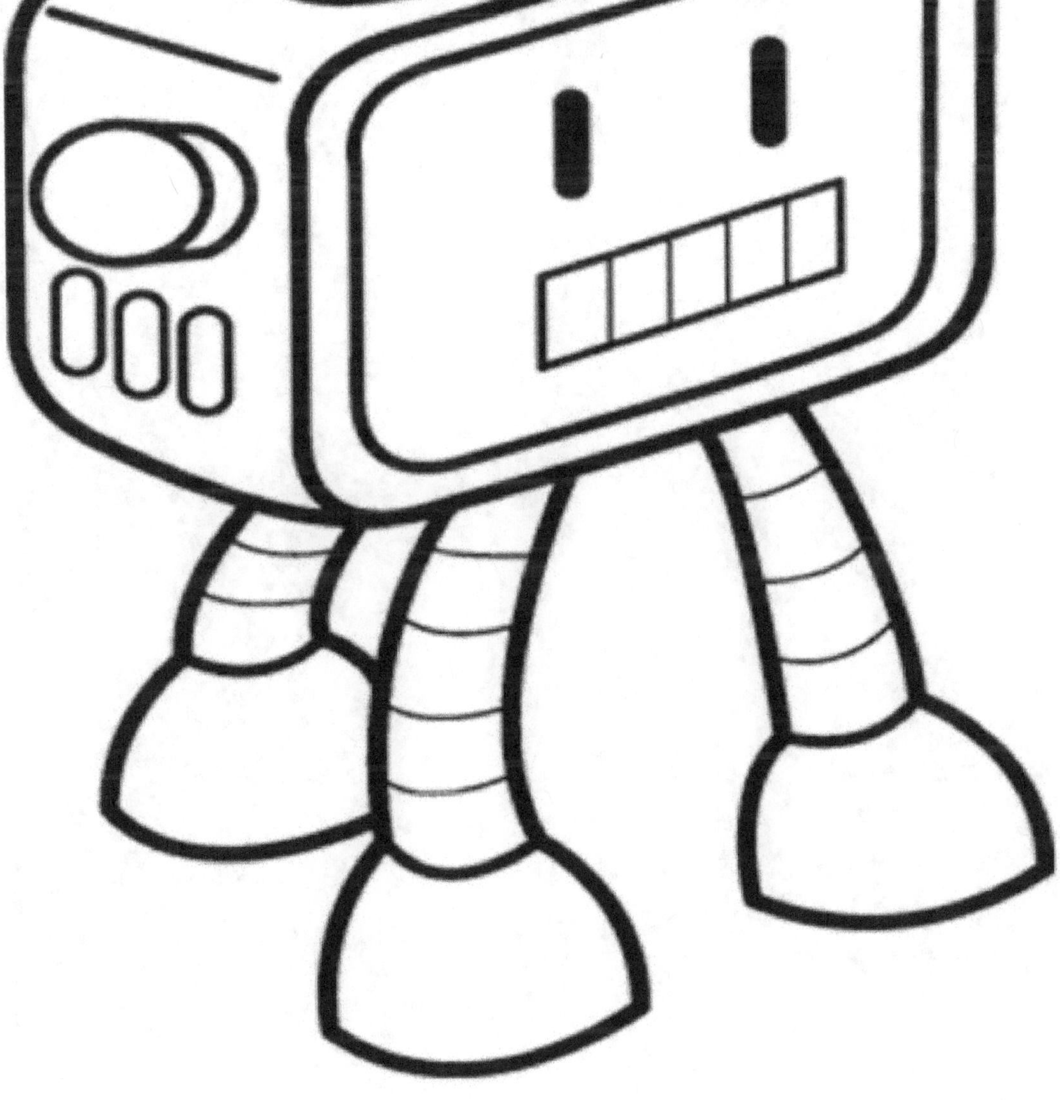

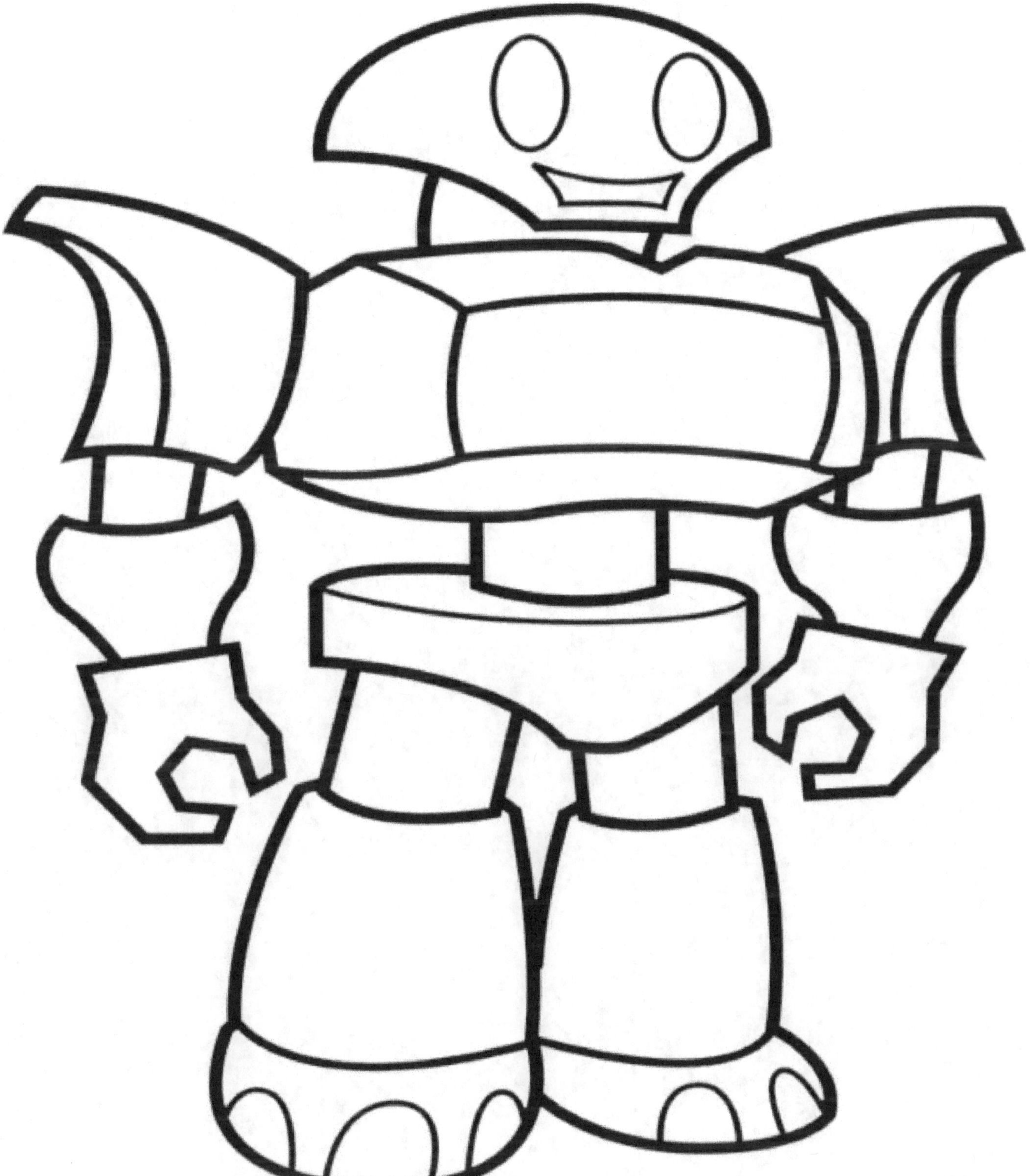

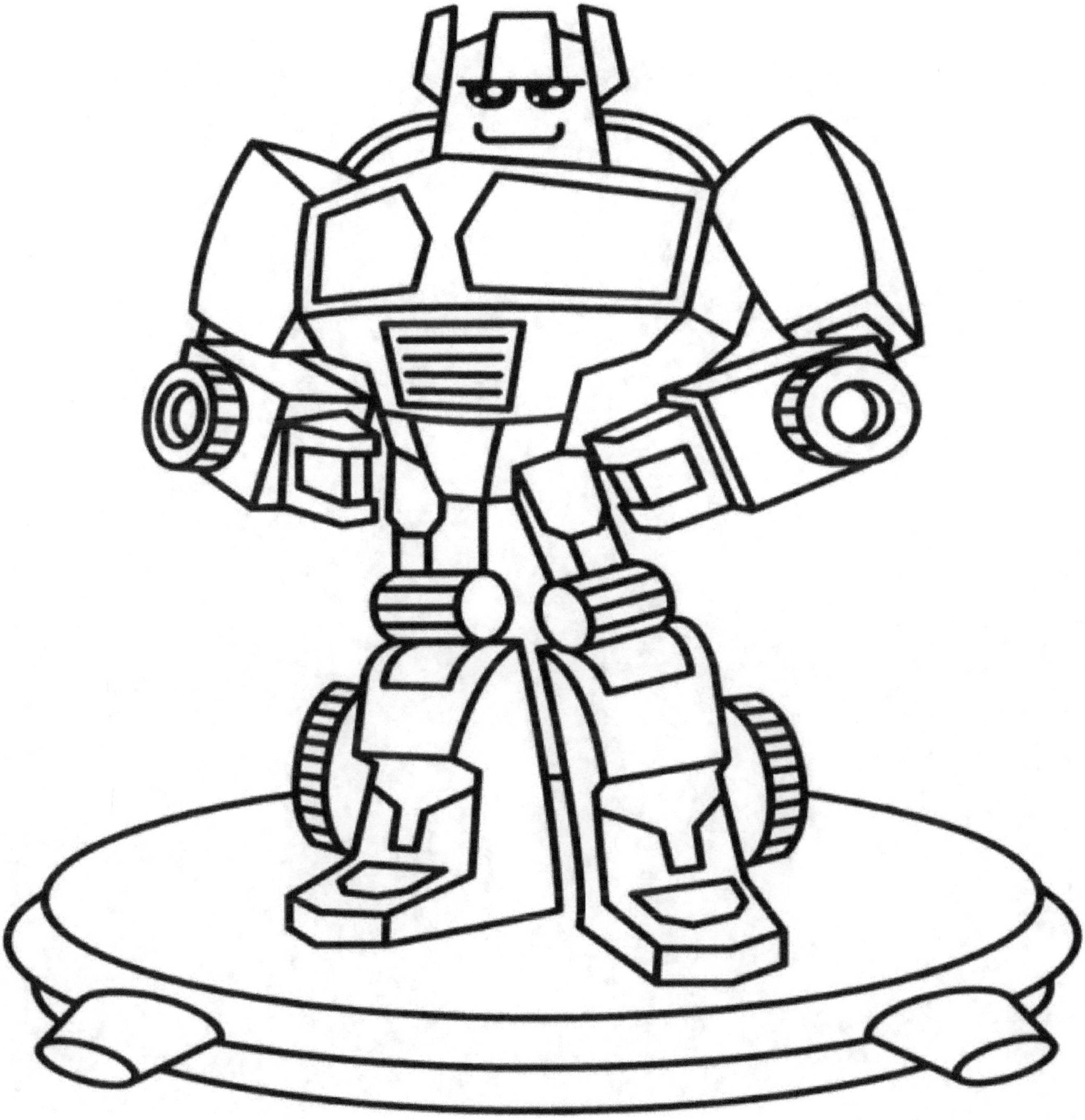

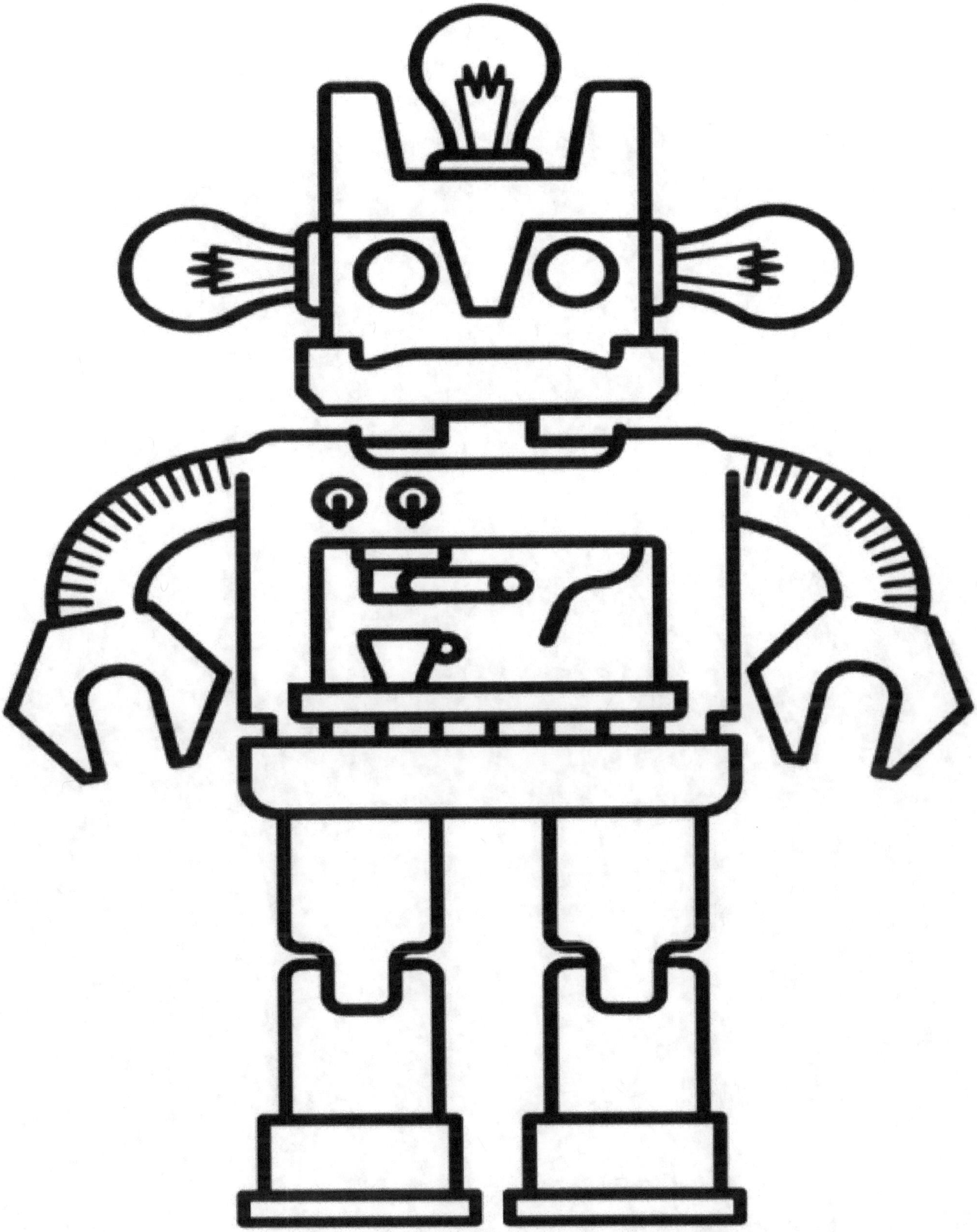

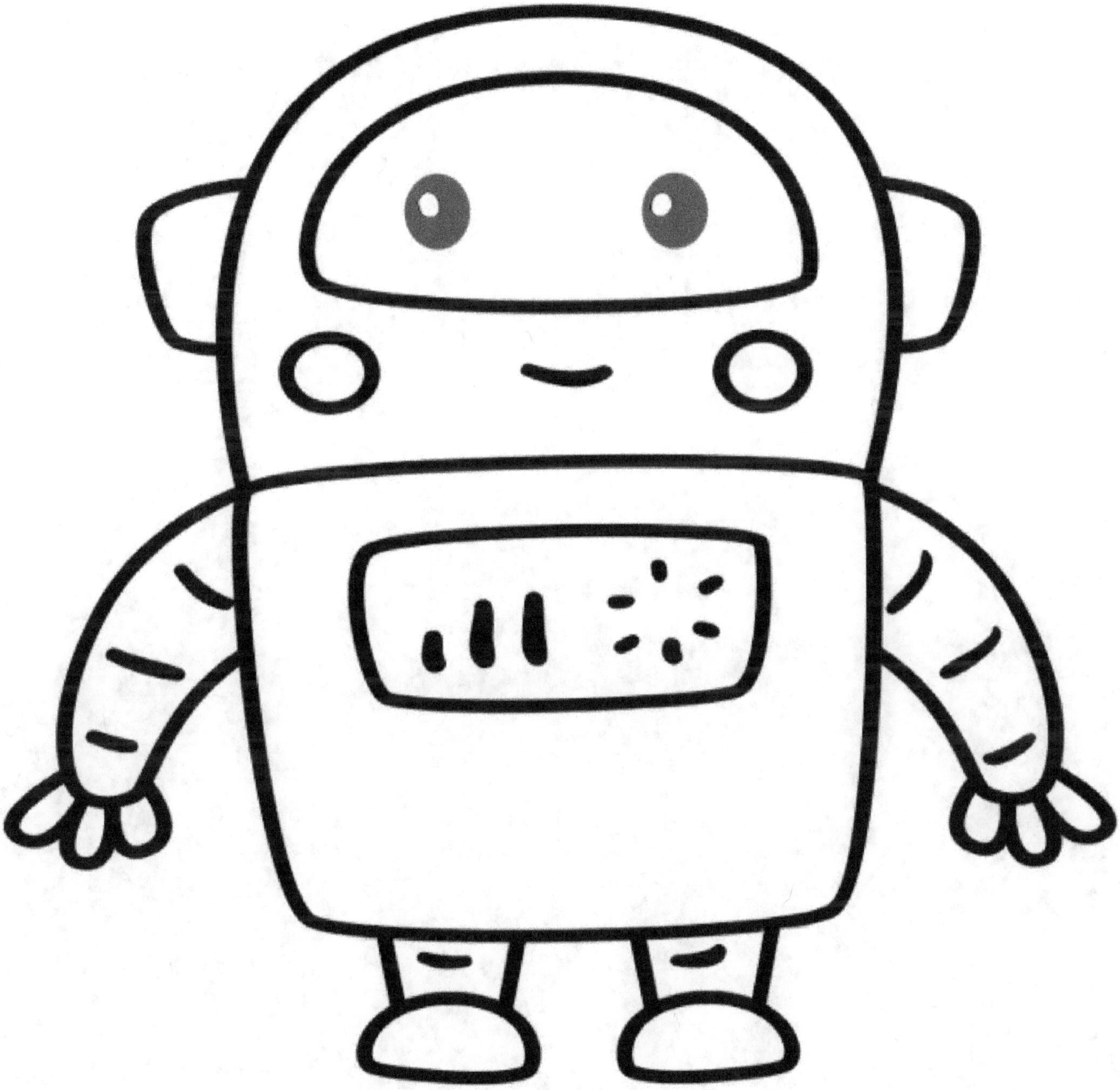

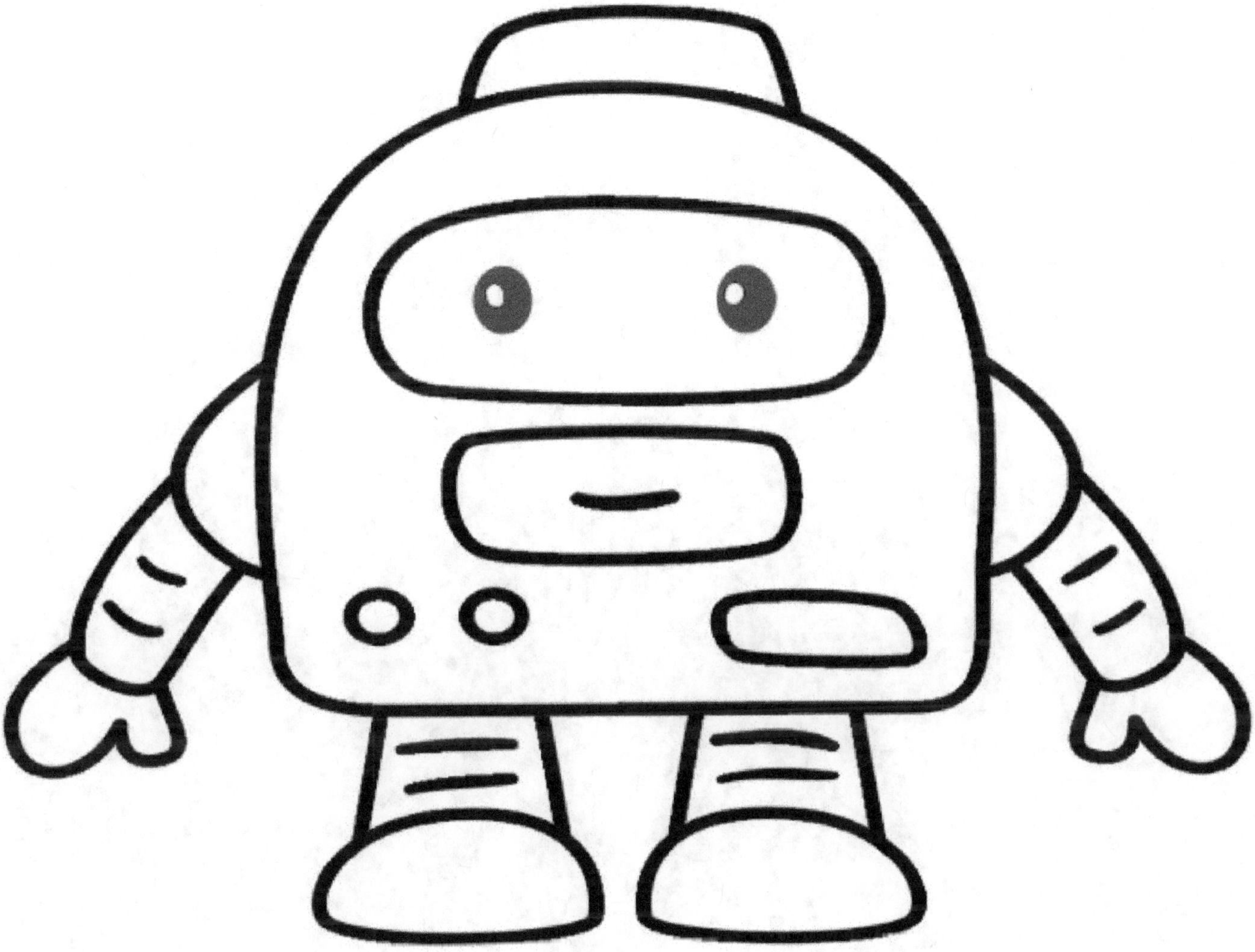

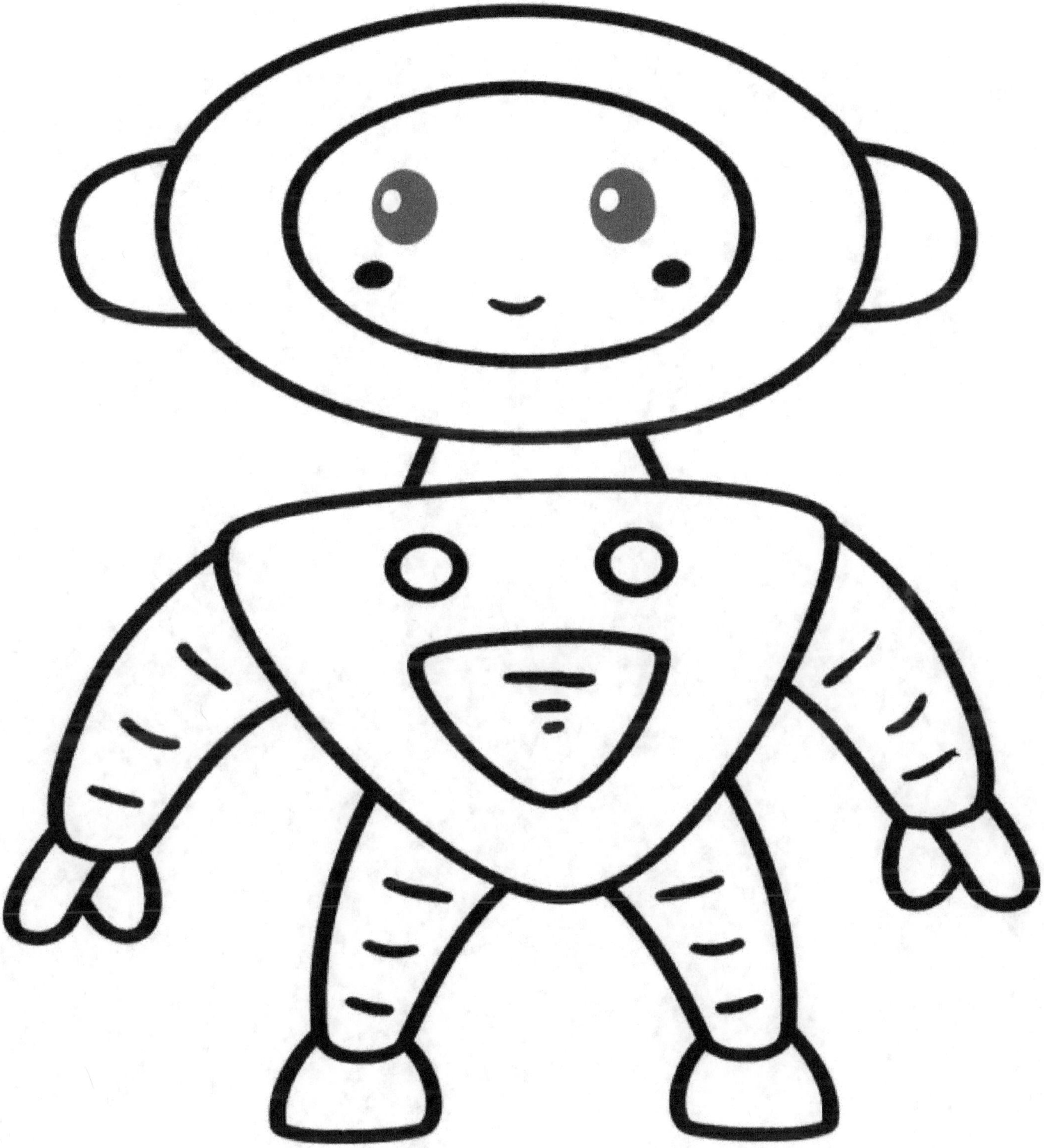

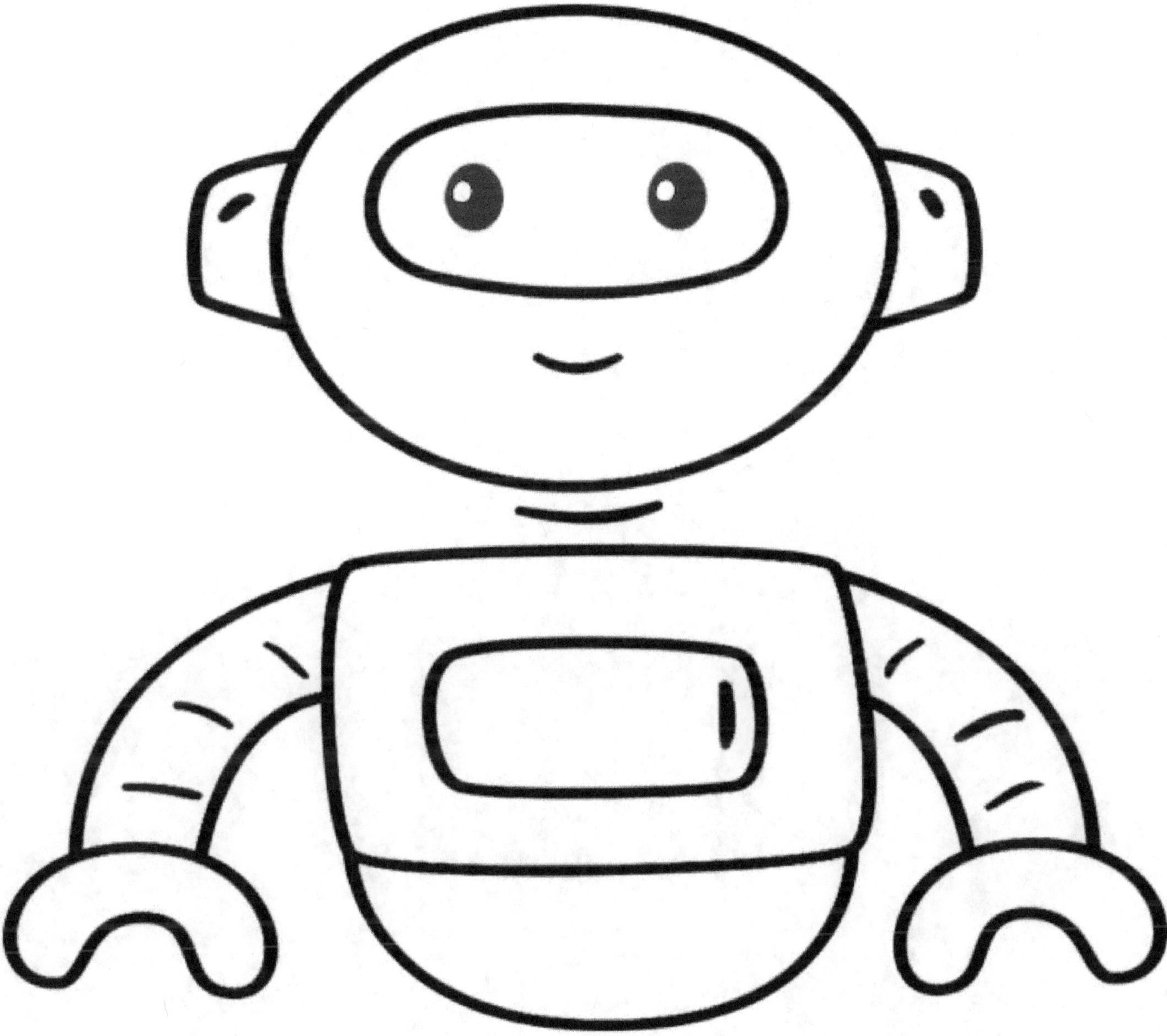

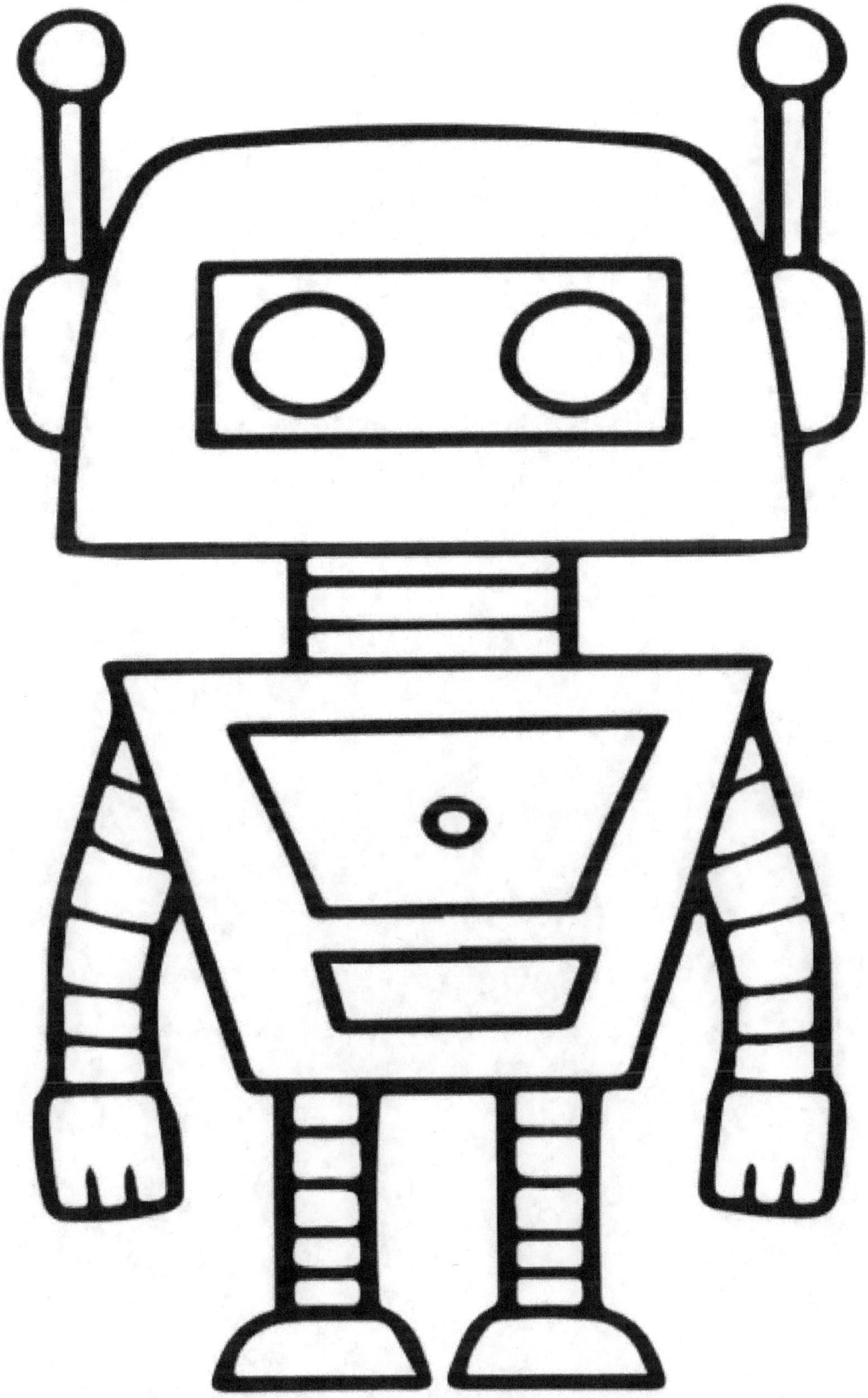

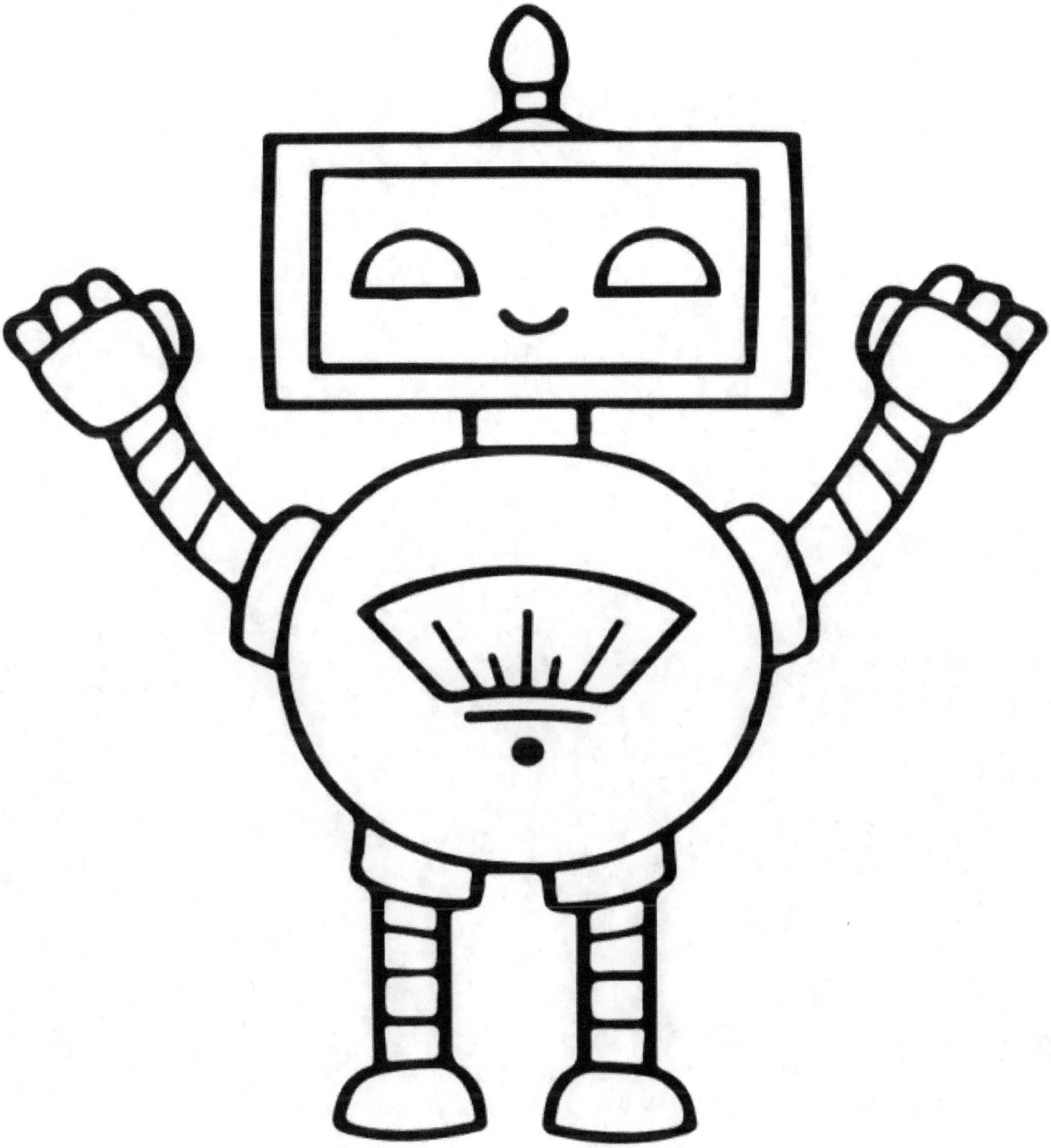

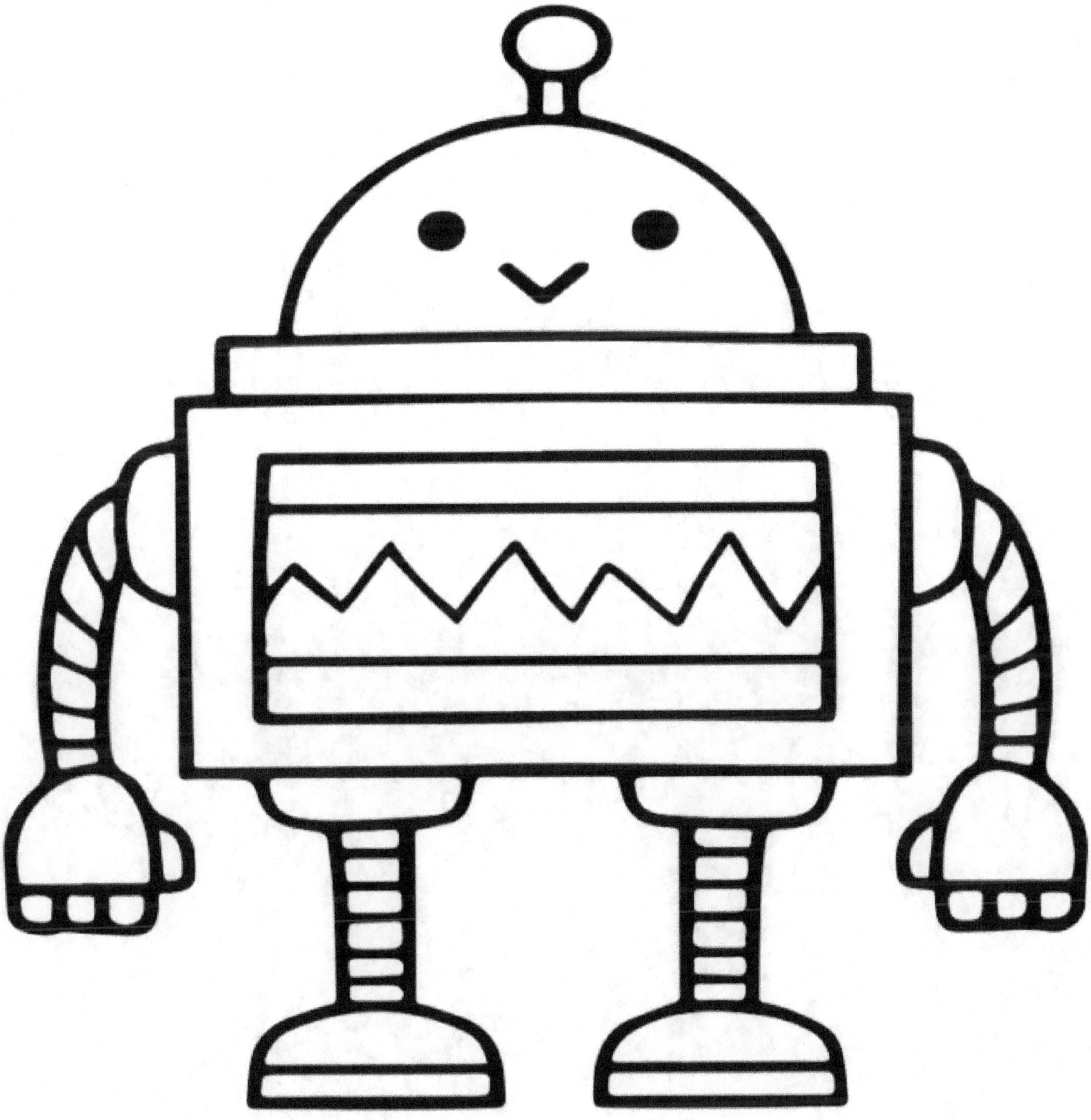

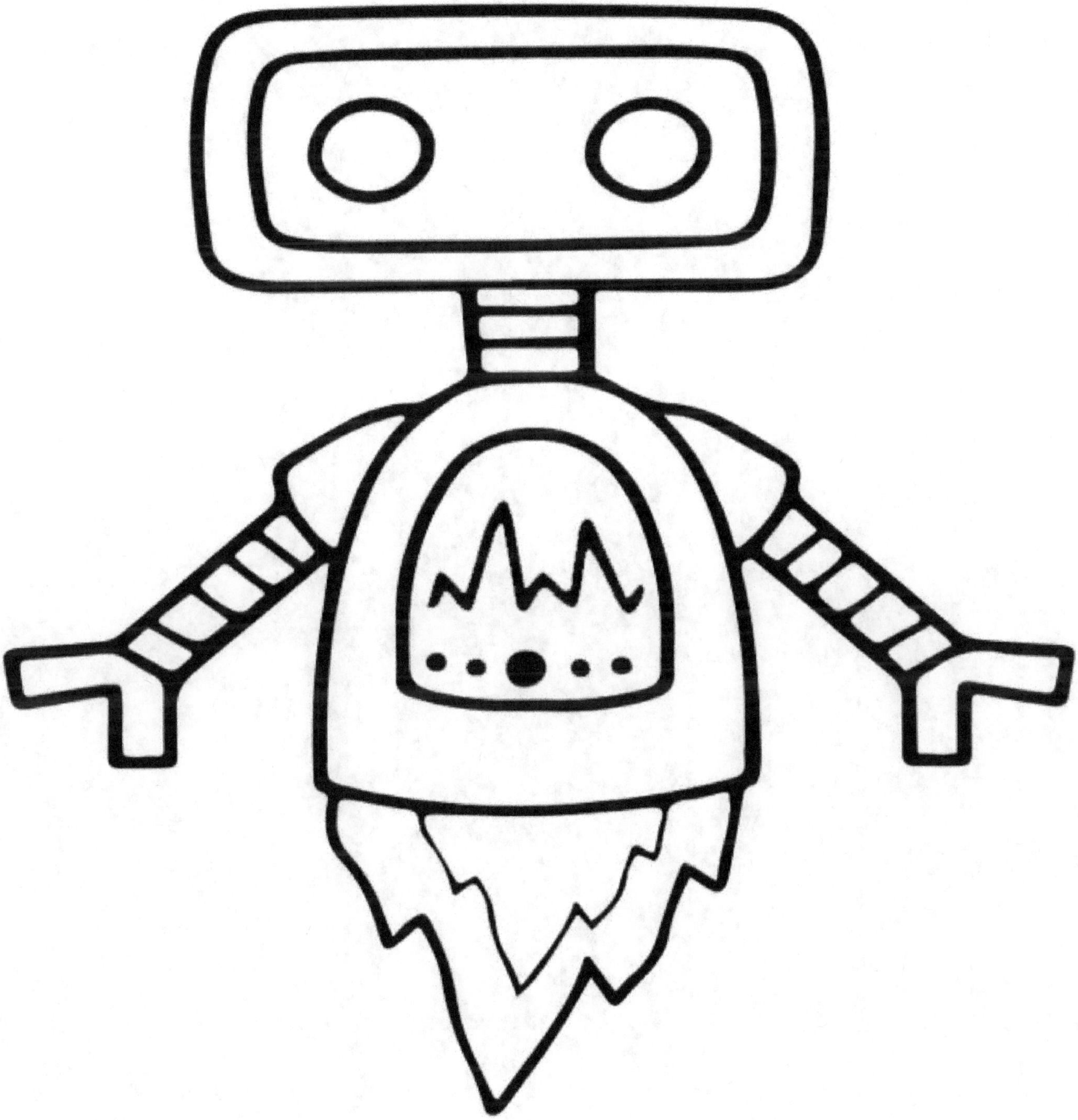

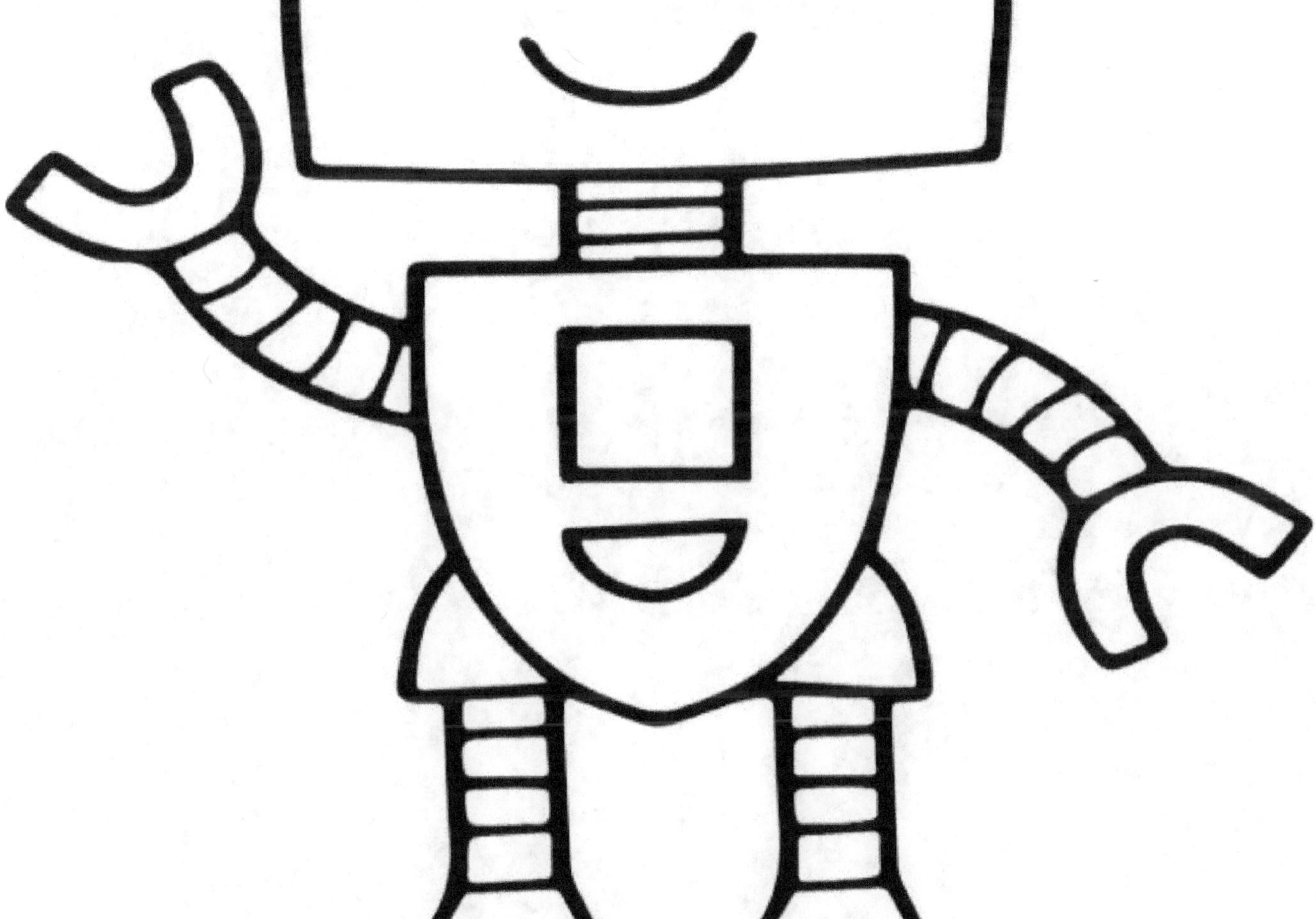

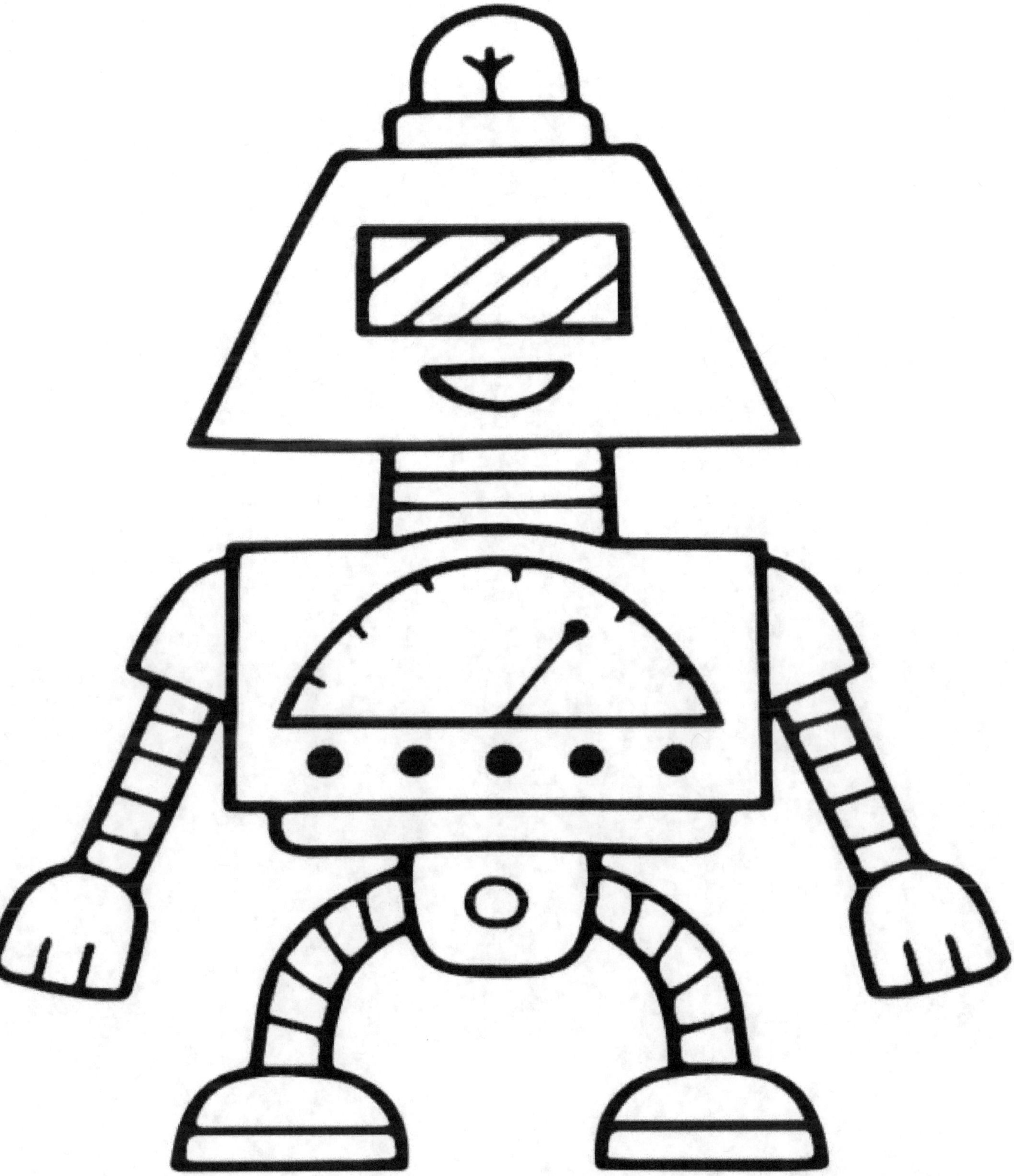

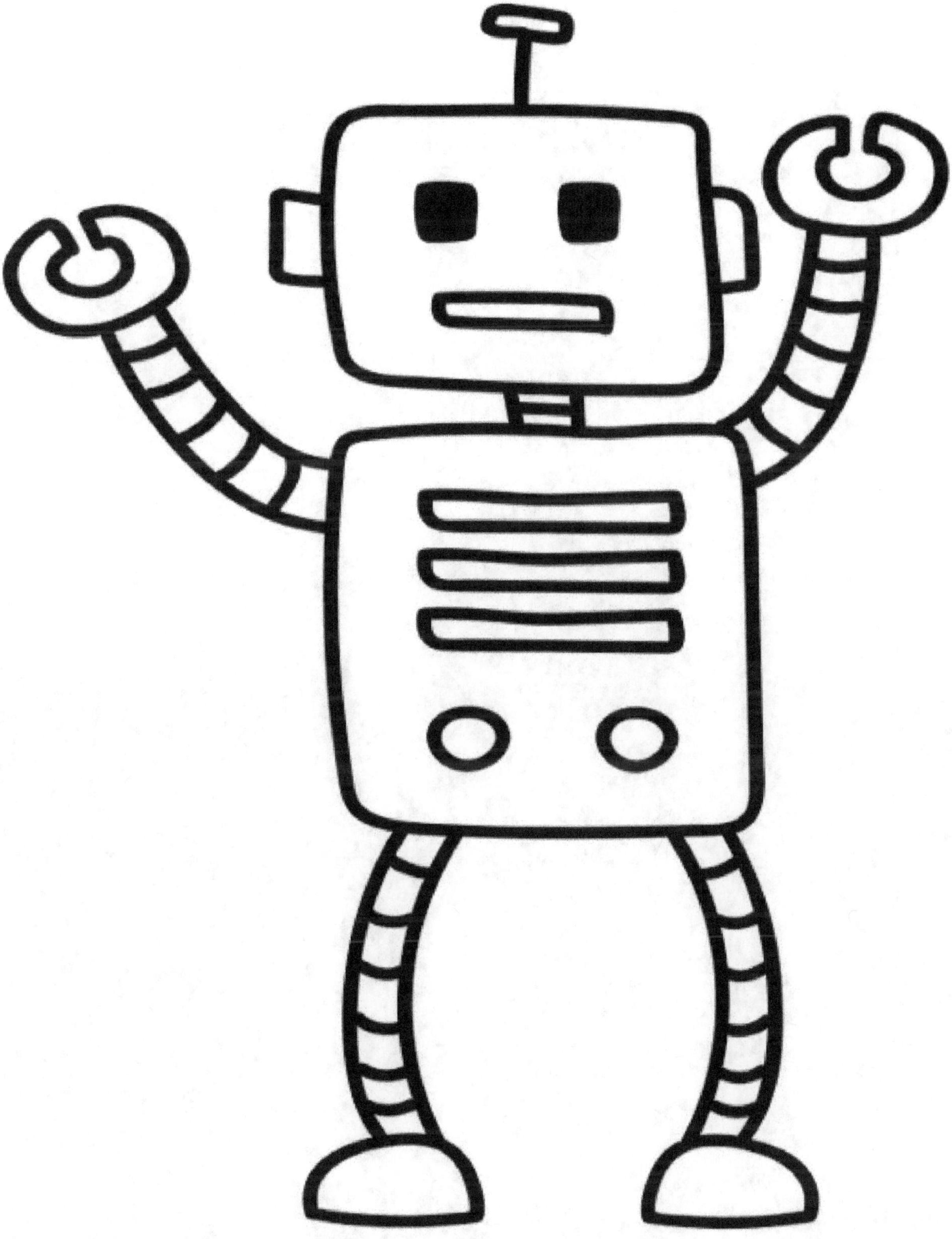

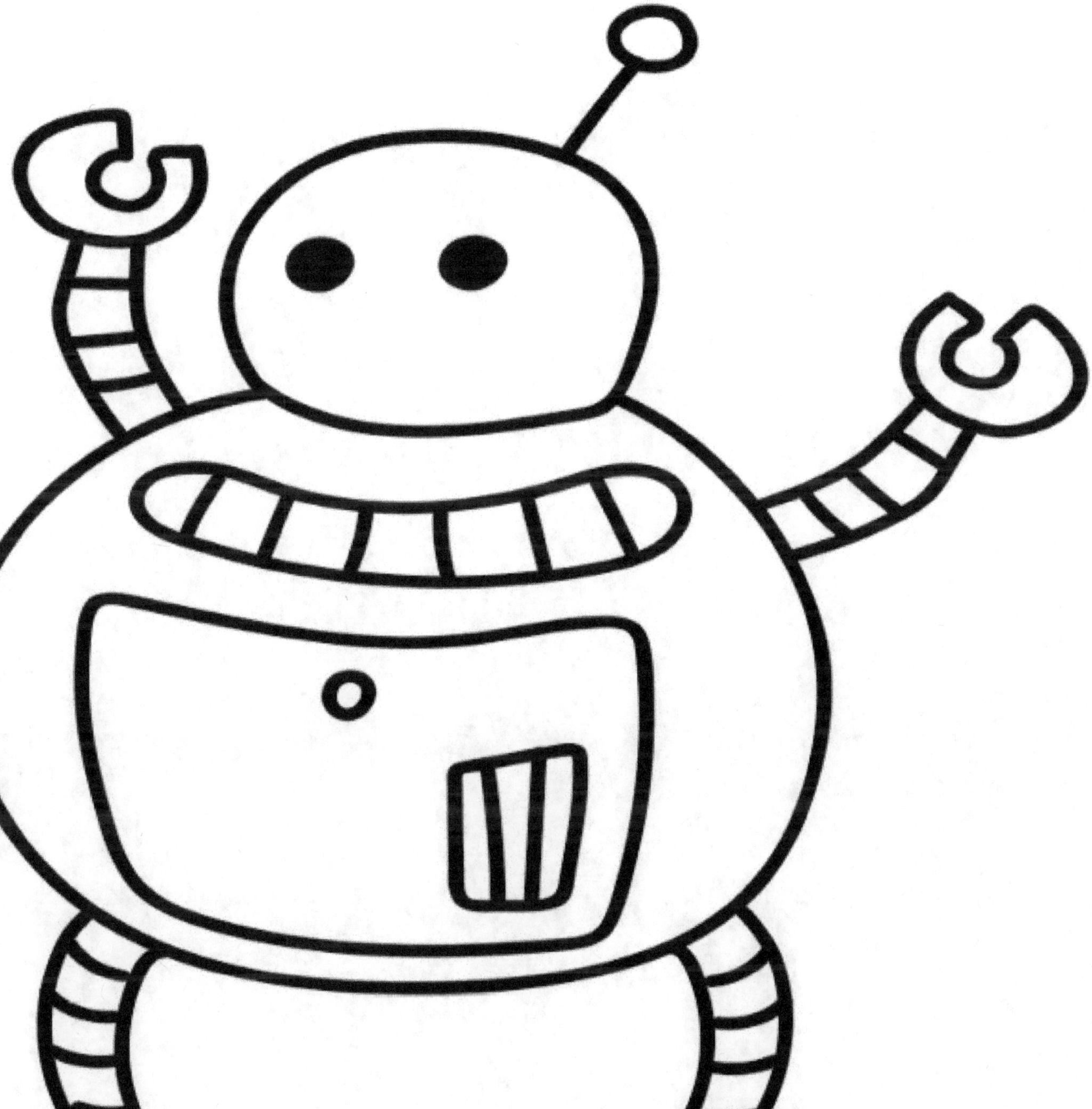

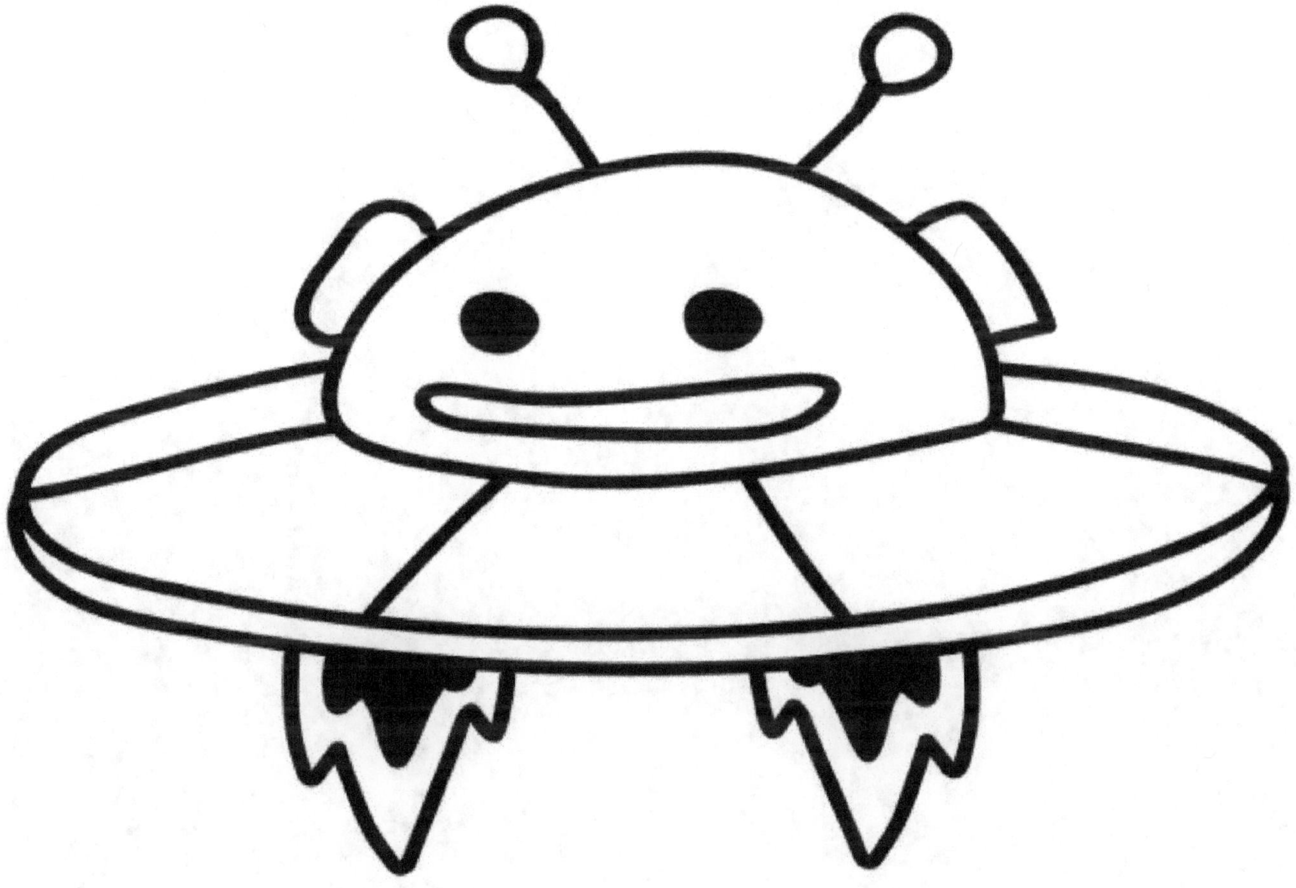

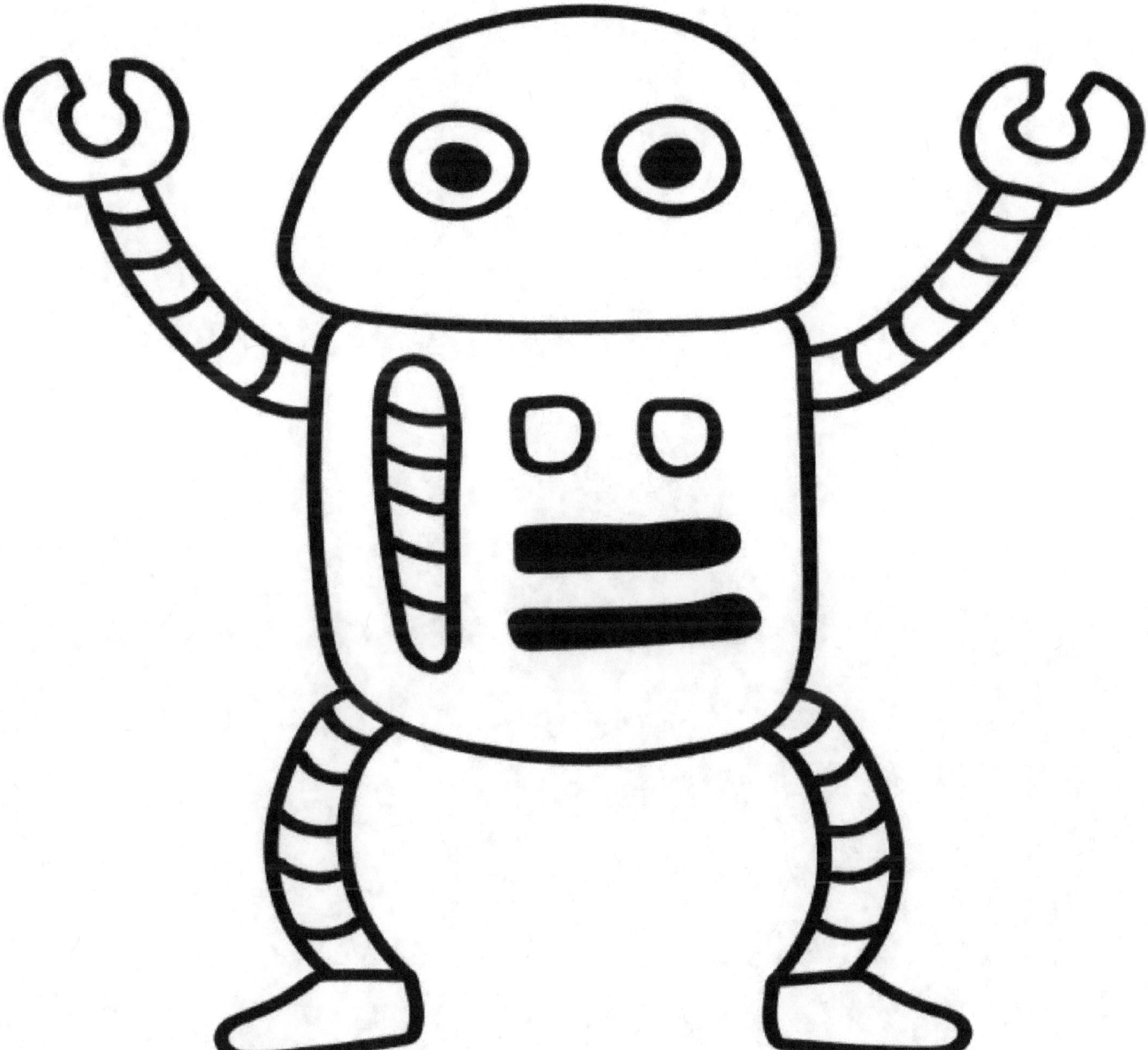

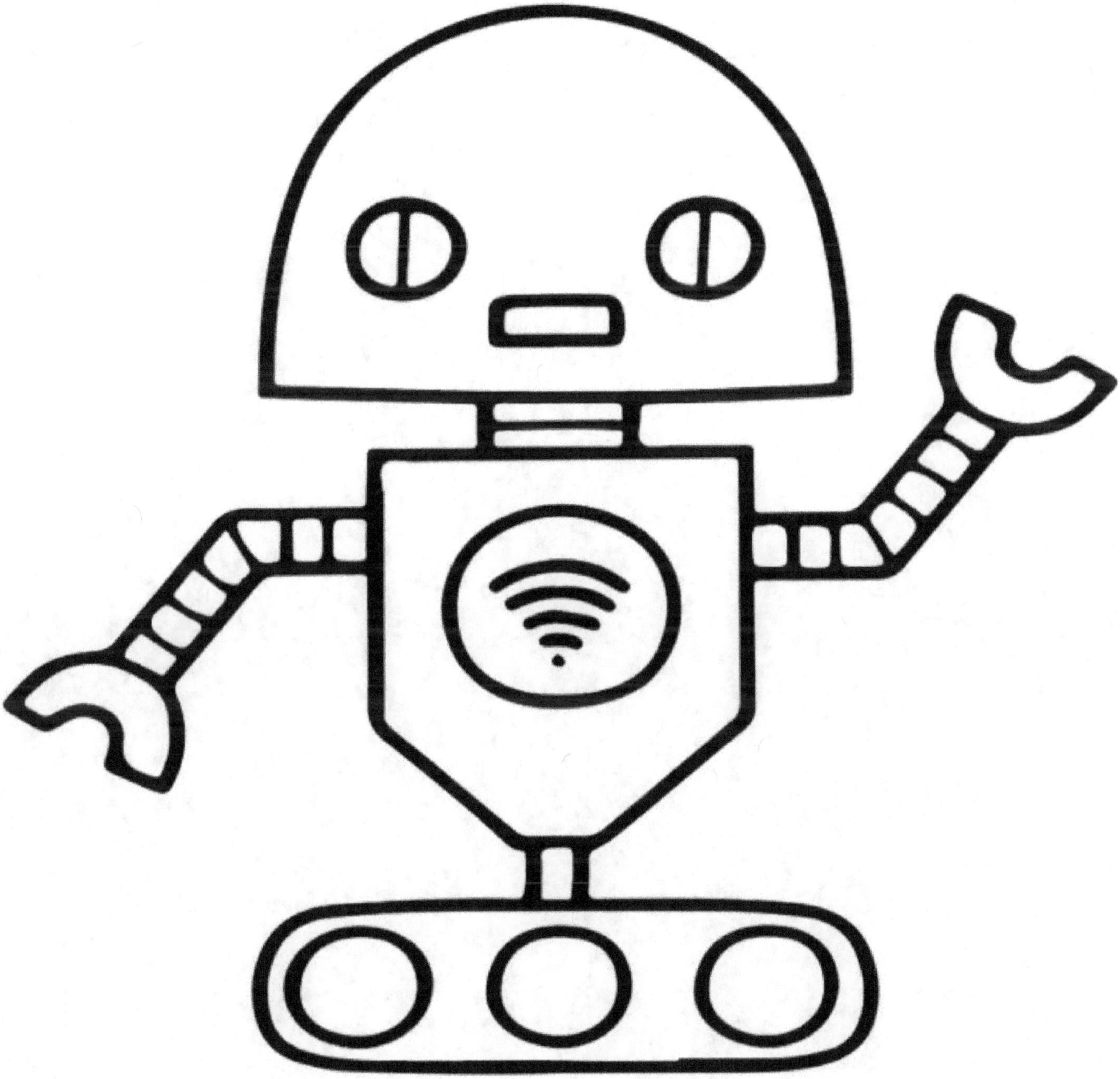

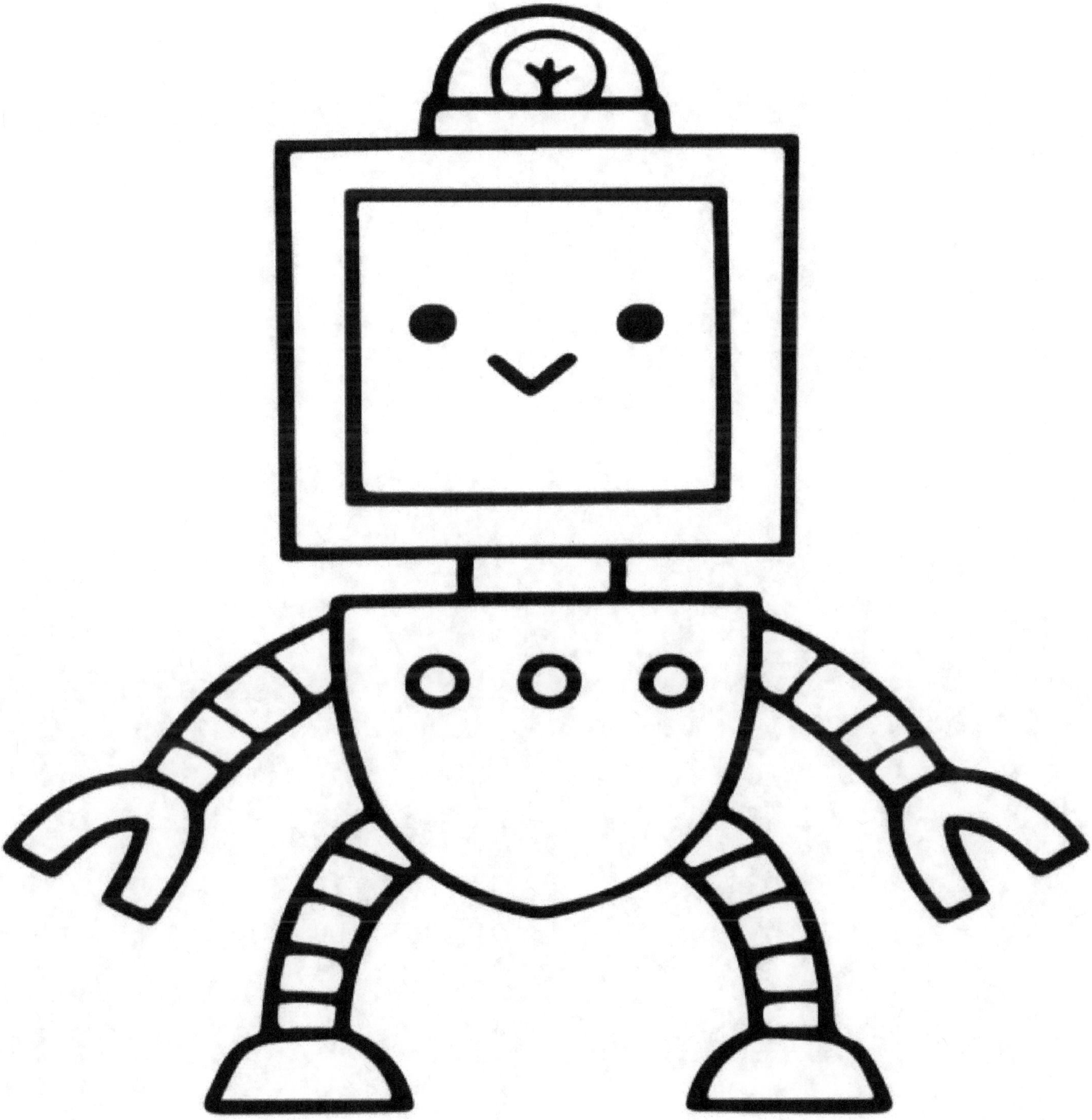

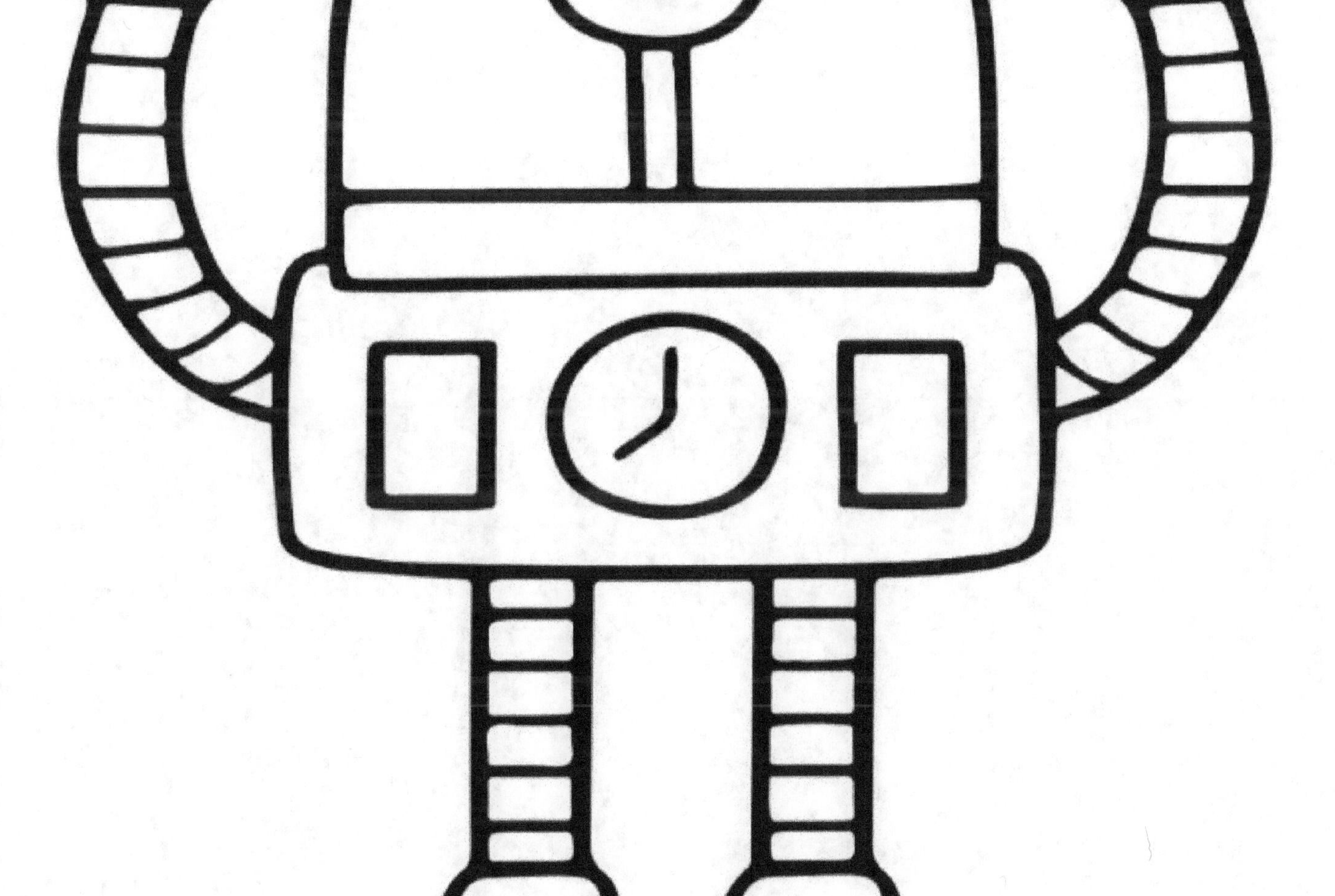

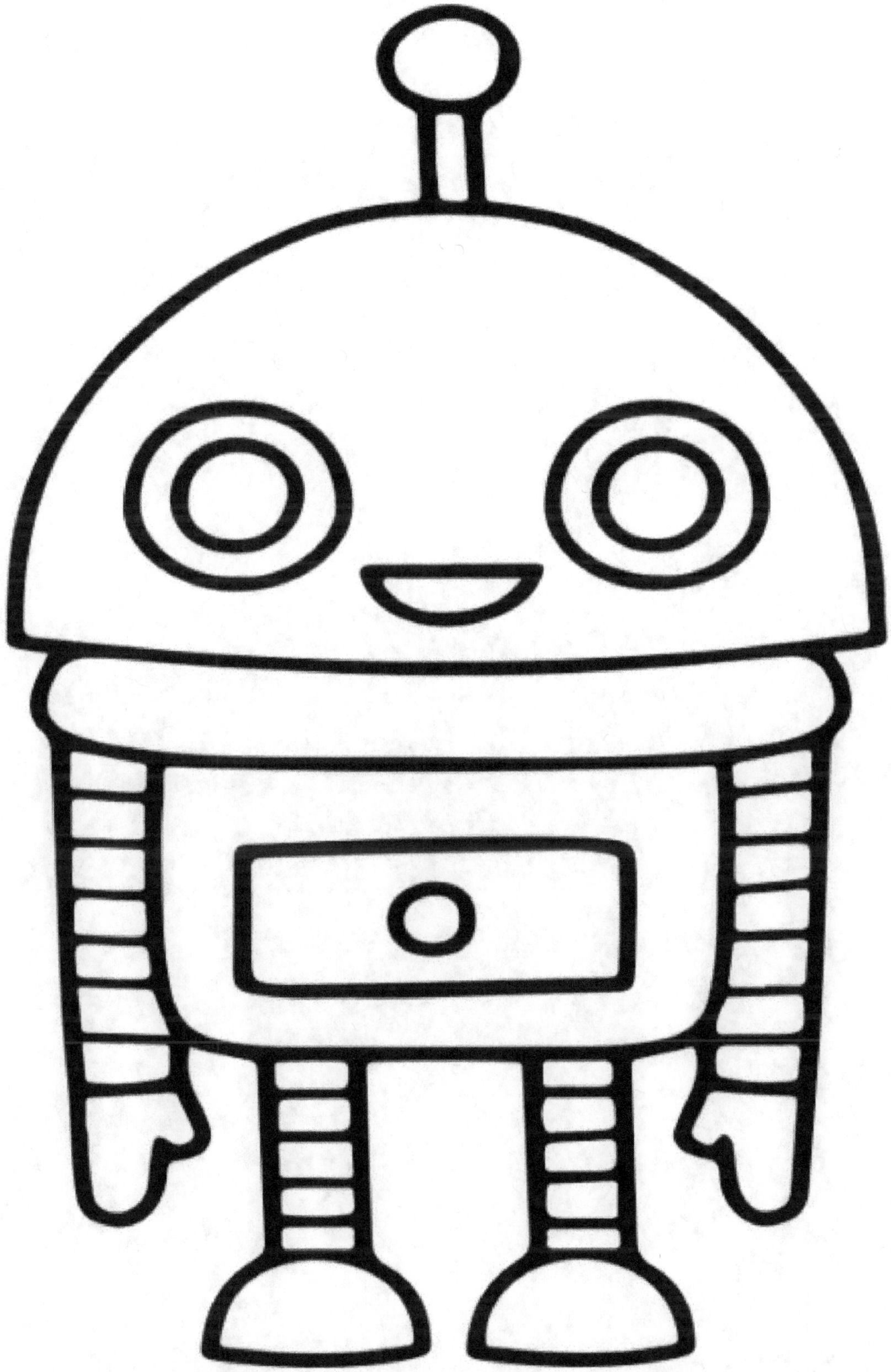

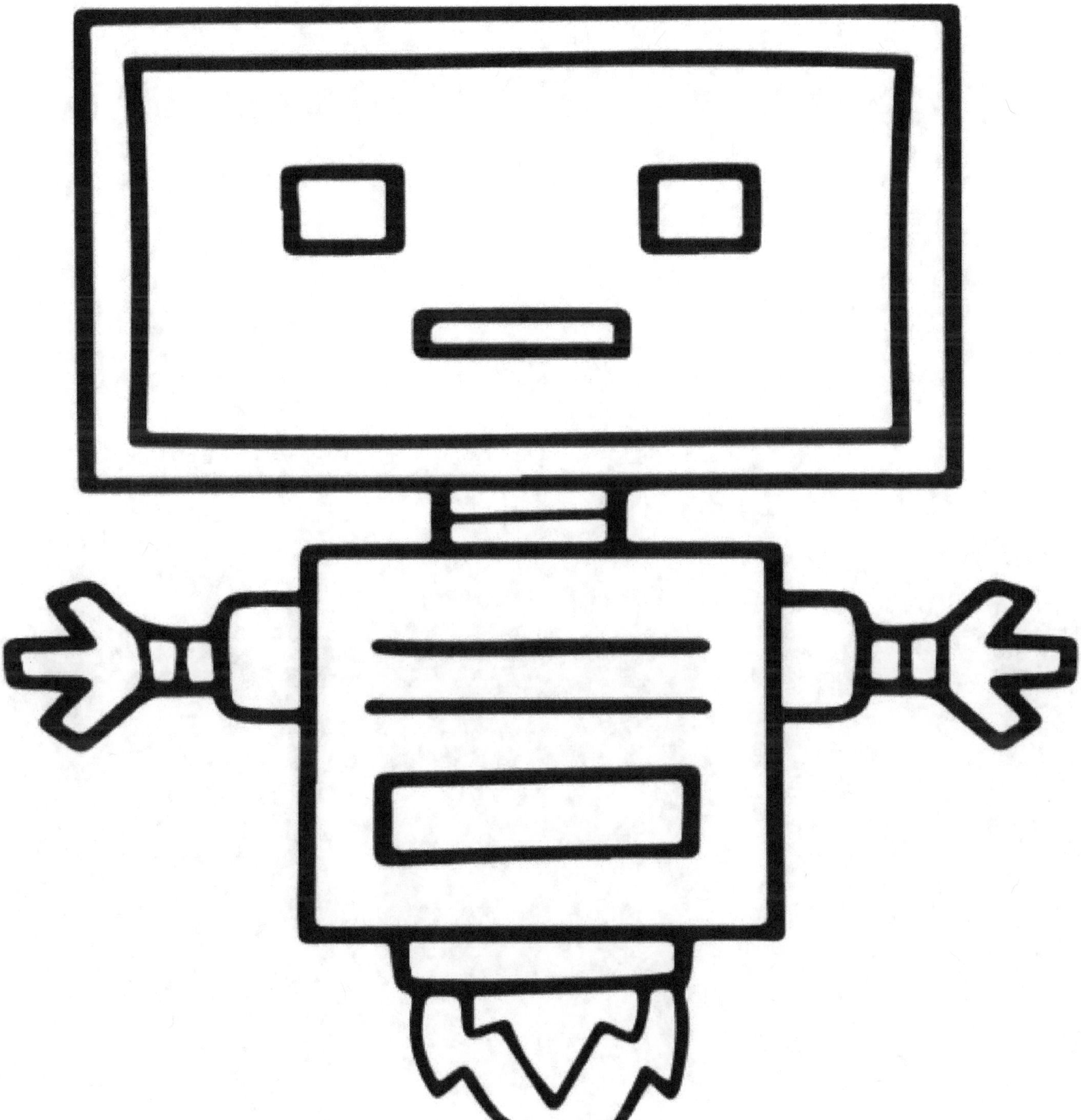

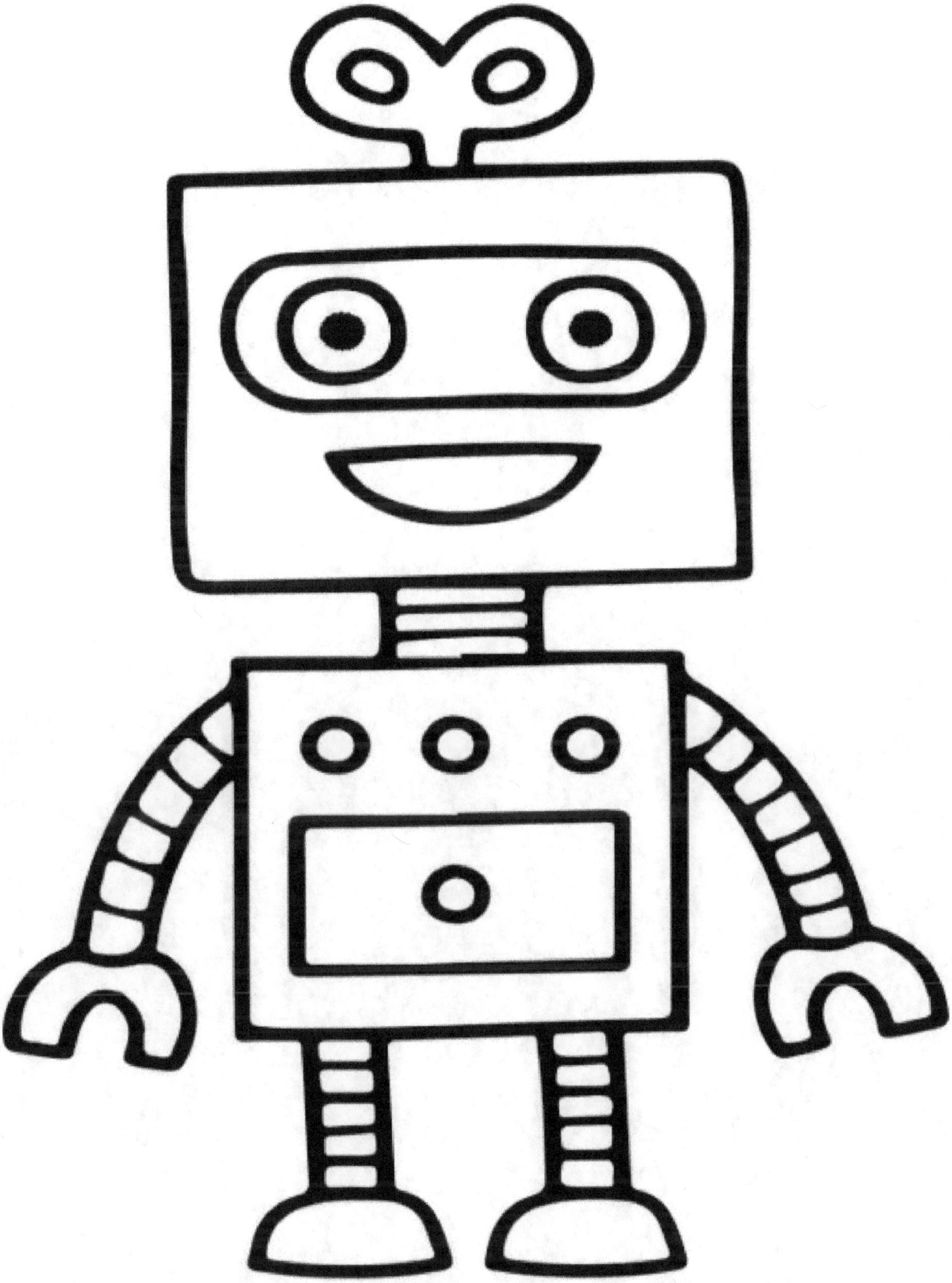

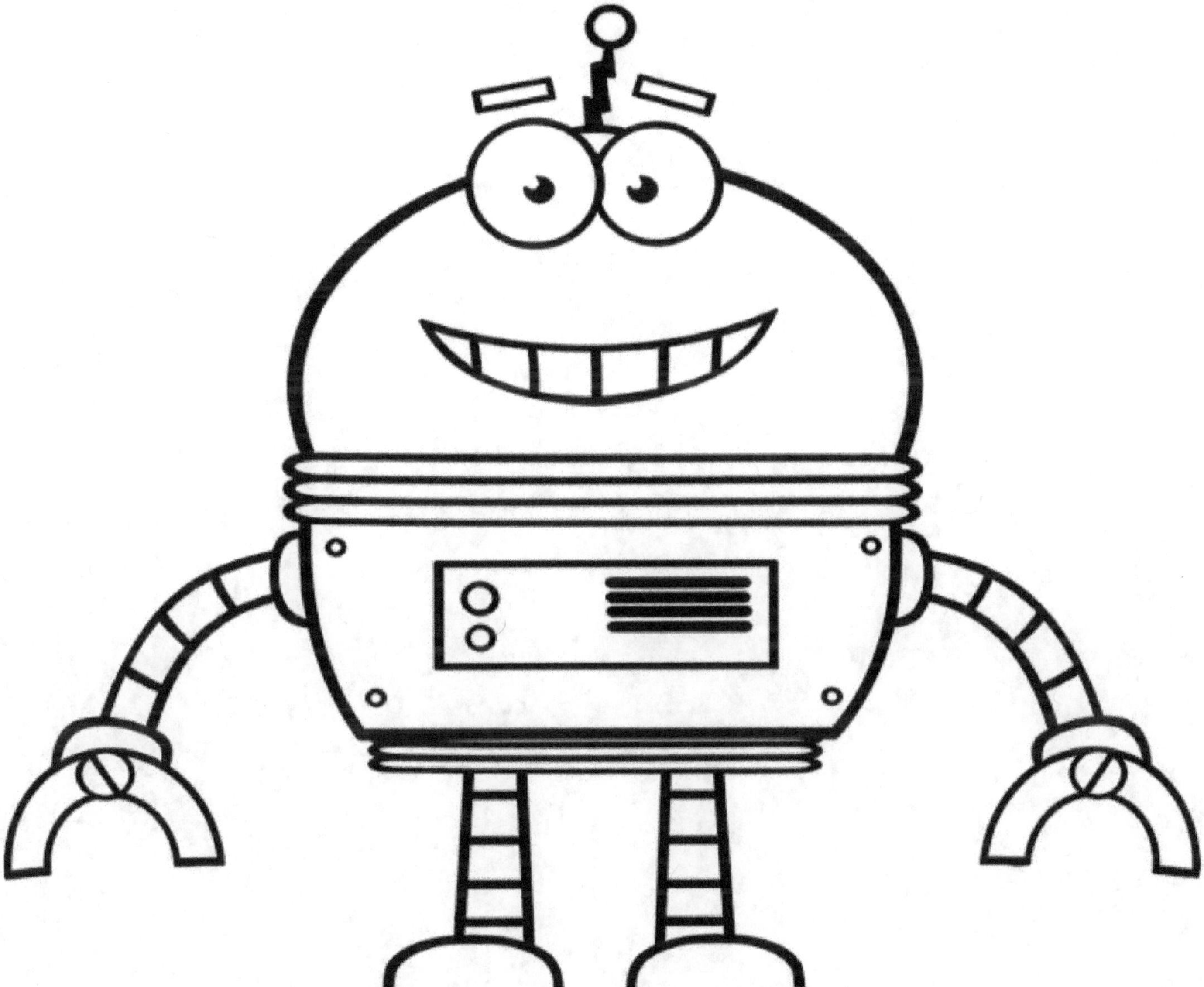

www.ingramcontent.com/pod-product-compliance
Lightning Source LLC
Chambersburg PA
CBHW082153230526
45467CB00044B/3223
* 9 7 8 1 7 1 0 5 9 7 5 7 8 *